Private Government

THE UNIVERSITY CENTER FOR HUMAN VALUES SERIES
STEPHEN MACEDO, EDITOR

A list of titles in this series appears at the back of the book.

Private Government

How Employers Rule Our Lives (and Why We Don't Talk about It)

Elizabeth Anderson

Introduction by
Stephen Macedo

Princeton University Press
Princeton and Oxford

Copyright © 2017 by Princeton University Press

Requests for permission to reproduce material from this work
should be sent to Permissions, Princeton University Press

Published by Princeton University Press,
41 William Street, Princeton, New Jersey 08540

In the United Kingdom: Princeton University Press,
6 Oxford Street, Woodstock, Oxfordshire OX20 1TR

press.princeton.edu

Jacket image courtesy of Shutterstock

All Rights Reserved

ISBN 978-0-691-17651-2

Library of Congress Control Number 2017933364

British Library Cataloging-in-Publication Data is available

This book has been composed in Adobe Text Pro and Helvetica Neue

Printed on acid-free paper. ∞

Printed in the United States of America

10 9 8 7 6 5 4 3 2 1

Contents

Introduction

Stephen Macedo

The two lectures that are the centerpiece of this volume call for a radical rethinking of the relationship between private enterprise and the freedom and dignity of workers. They describe—in broad but vivid brushstrokes—a centuries-long decline in free market progressivism. They argue that, from the time of the English Civil War, in the mid-seventeenth century, to Abraham Lincoln, two hundred years later, there were good grounds for optimism about the capacity of free markets to promote equality of status and standing. That optimism gave way—with the Industrial Revolution, and for reasons described later—to pessimism concerning rising inequality and domination in the workplace. As opportunities for self-employment declined drastically, workers had fewer alternatives to managers' arbitrary and unaccountable authority. The breadth of that authority is extremely wide, leaving workers vulnerable to being fired for speech and conduct far removed from their workplaces. Today's free market thinking—among scholars, intellectuals, and politicians—radically misconstrues the condition of most private sector workers and is blind to the degree of arbitrary and unaccountable power to which private sector workers are subject.

Just how this happened is the subject of Elizabeth Anderson's important and timely Tanner Lectures on Human Values, first delivered at Princeton University in early 2014. Anderson is one of the world's foremost political philosophers: the author of widely influential books on *Values in Ethics and Economics* (1993) and *The Imperative of Integration* (2010). Among her many articles, the pathbreaking "What Is the Point of Equality?" (1999) shifted the attention of social philosophers beyond a sole focus on inequalities in material distribution toward equality in social relations. Professor Anderson's long-standing concerns with social equality of authority, esteem, and standing are at the center of this book.

The two lectures are followed by four pointed commentaries originally delivered, and revised for publication, by eminent scholars who draw on their expertise in history, literature, political theory, economics, and philosophy. The volume ends with Professor Anderson's response to the challenges of her critics.

The remainder of this introduction offers a brief overview of each of these contributions.

In her first lecture, Elizabeth Anderson argues that free market political and economic theory—nowadays associated with libertarians and the political right—originated as an egalitarian and progressive agenda: from the Levellers in England in the seventeenth century through the American Civil War, "market society" was often understood "as a free society of equals." Anderson ably sketches the highlights of the free market egalitarianism of the early modern period, focusing on the Levellers, John Locke, Adam Smith, and Thomas Paine, among others.

Economic liberties and free markets were opposed to social hierarchies in the economy, politics, religion, society, and the family. As she nicely summarizes:

> Opposition to economic monopolies was part of a broader agenda of dismantling monopolies across all domains of social life: not just the guilds, but monopolies of church and press, monopolization of the vote by the rich, and monopolization of family power by men. Eliminate monopoly, and far more people would be able to attain personal independence and become masterless men and women.

It was only in the nineteenth century that free market thinking drifted away from its earlier egalitarian moorings. Following Paine, free market thinkers increasingly regarded the state as an abuser of power in the name of special interests. The other cause was the Industrial Revolution.

In the seventeenth and eighteenth centuries, thinkers such as the Leveller John Lilburne and the great political economist Adam Smith assumed that free men operating in free markets would be independent artisans, merchants, or participants in small-scale manufacturing enterprises. Smith's "pin factory"—which illustrated the division of labor—had ten employees. Thomas Paine and the American Founders, who favored economic as well as political liberty, assumed that the bulk of the population would be self-employed. In late eighteenth- and early nineteenth-century America "free market wages were high" given "chronic labor shortages," and "self-employment was a ready option for nearly all" white men. Thus, it made sense to equate economic liberty, free markets, and independence.

Free market egalitarians of old were, moreover, far from doctrinaire libertarians in their policy proposals. Many, like

Smith and Paine, advocated public education, and Paine "proposed a system of universal social insurance, including old-age pensions, survivor benefits, and disability payments for families whose members could not work," as well as a universal system of stakeholder grants.

Summing up the free market egalitarianism of the seventeenth to the mid-nineteenth centuries, Anderson observes that

> Smith's greatest hope—the hope shared by labor radicals from the Levellers to the Chartists, from Paine to Lincoln—was that freeing up markets would dramatically expand the ranks of the self-employed, who would exercise talent and judgment in governing their own productive activities, independent of micromanaging bosses.

The Industrial Revolution dramatically altered the assumptions upon which free market egalitarianism had rested. "Economies of scale overwhelmed the economy of small proprietors," and "opportunities for self-employment shrank dramatically." It "dramatically widened the gulf between employers and employees in manufacturing," and, in addition, "ranks within the firm multiplied."

The radical changes wrought by the Industrial Revolution for most workers, and the consequent mismatch between free market theory and reality, gave rise, says Anderson, to a "symbiotic relationship between libertarianism and authoritarianism that blights our political discourse to this day."

In her second lecture, Anderson advances her central and most arresting claim: that the modern industrial firm amounts to a system of arbitrary and unaccountable "private government" and "dictatorship":

Most workers in the United States are governed by communist dictatorships in their work lives. Usually, those dictatorships have the legal authority to regulate workers' off-hour lives as well—their political activities, speech, choice of sexual partner, use of recreational drugs, alcohol, smoking, and exercise. . . . [M]ost employers exercise this off-hours authority irregularly, arbitrarily, and without warning. . . . [O]nly about half of U.S. workers enjoy even partial protection of their off-duty speech from employer meddling.

Anderson argues that private government exists when people are subject, in some part of their lives, to authorities that can order them around and impose sanctions for noncompliance. In the workplace, moreover, governing authorities have arbitrary and unaccountable power over workers. Libertarians and free market economists and politicians wrongly equate "freedom" with private enterprise, ignoring the reality that for most workers, employment in large firms brings with it subjection to arbitrary power that extends beyond their work lives. Anderson insists that most Americans and many others radically misunderstand the nature of liberty and its opposites: domination and dictatorship. Just as the security of private property depends upon a strong state, so too do many forms of freedom.

Current theories of the firm help explain why large-scale enterprises exist and are constituted by hierarchies of authority. As Anderson observes, "Efficient employment contracts are . . . necessarily incomplete," managers must have discretion to coordinate workers' activities. But these theories do not explain the breadth of employers' authority over workers' lives. "Under the employment-at-will baseline, workers, in effect, cede *all* of their rights to their employers, except those specifically guaranteed to them by law, for the duration of the employ-ment relationship." The result is that "Employers' authority over workers, outside of collective bargaining and a few other contexts . . . is sweeping, arbitrary, and unaccountable—not subject to notice, process, or appeal." Workplace governance "is a form of private government," underwritten by law.

Of course, if workers object to the conditions of their em-ployment, they can quit. But the costs of exit for many workers are extremely high. To deny employers' authority over workers because of freedom of exit, says Anderson, "is like saying that Mussolini wasn't a dictator, because Italians could emigrate." Libertarian-leaning thinkers and politicians are, says Anderson, blind to the real nature of employment because they implicitly carry over assumptions that held only before the Industrial Rev-olution, when self-employment and economic independence were within reach of most workers.

As she concludes her indictment of today's free market thinking, Anderson allows that private governments in the economy lack many of the directly coercive powers of actual states, and they often refrain from exercising much of their power over workers' lives, especially the lives of higher income and skilled workers. Nevertheless, the fact remains that "the constitution of workplace government is both arbitrary and dictatorial," and that it "is not dictated by efficiency or freedom of contract, but rather by the state."

Anderson closes by suggesting a variety of ways to increase worker protections against arbitrary treatment: these include enhanced exit rights, a workers' bill of rights, and greater "voice," including via improved legal support for unions and collective bargaining. Most importantly, our public discourse should rec-ognize the reality of workers' subjection to arbitrary private government in the workplace and explore ways of remedying it.

The first of our four commentators, Ann Hughes, a leading historian of early modern England and the English Civil War, and Professor of Early Modern History at Keele University in the UK, applauds as "exemplary" Anderson's "deployment of historical material as a storehouse of imagination, and a legacy to the present." She notes recent invocations of the Levellers by progressives in Britain and elsewhere, but she also advances a "darker" and more complex view of seventeenth-century England. She emphasizes, for one thing, that the effects of the burgeoning market order were various, and far from uniformly positive: inequality and social polarization increased, and substantial portions of the population depended sometimes or often on public assistance.

Hughes also emphasizes that the Levellers were far from radically egalitarian by our standards, with many excluding from suffrage beggars as well as servants and apprentices, and women. She suggests that free market thinking was not foundational to the Levellers, but rather "deduced from other elements of social life," and also that the "economic and social implications of market relations were already—long before the industrial revolution—less benevolent than Adam Smith and Professor Anderson believe."

Market relations themselves were complex, depending on the social phenomena of trust and credit, and market principles were tempered by "a sense of collective and communal activism," as well as deference to some customary rights. Finally, Hughes emphasizes that the Levellers continued to fall back on "a conception of society as made up of male-headed households, with women as valued but subordinate participants," further complicating claims about early modern egalitarianism.

David Bromwich, Sterling Professor of English at Yale University and author of many works on politics, political theory, and history, asks how the optimism about economic liberty and market society of the seventeenth century gave way to the pessimism Professor Anderson describes. He agrees with Anderson that "political theory should not stop at the door of the workplace," but he doubts that the idea of market freedom, as developed by Adam Smith and others, ever furnished a sufficient basis for political freedom and democratic equality. Bromwich argues that Smith understood that "self-interest" would operate for "the long-term good of society . . . almost independent of the will" of social and political actors. He suggests that "Thomas Paine—a radical democrat through and through . . . may belong in a different history": he believed in markets but his vision "was essentially political and only secondarily economic."

Bromwich allows, with Smith, that the extension of markets raises the level of material well-being of all, including of the poorest. It may even transpire that, as Smith bragged, "an industrious and frugal peasant" in commercial society could enjoy an "accommodation" that greatly exceeds that of "an African king, the absolute master of the lives and liberties of ten thousand naked savages." And yet, Bromwich observes, "the African king has *power*, and with his power, a fearlessness of misery, which is denied to the European peasant." He worries that Anderson underrates "the difference between political power and market equality."

Bromwich ends by raising concerns about the sort of world in which everything—including labor itself—becomes a commodity. Quoting Oliver Goldsmith, he worries about the human costs of market dislocations for traditional societies: "trade uproots lives and turns ancient occupations obsolete." Quoting Karl Polanyi, 170 years later, Bromwich worries about the ever more complete commodification of man and nature. He ends by thanking Anderson for encouraging us to "think closely again about the early modern theories of equality and freedom that rationalize but do not justify our own market society."

Our third commentator, the philosopher Niko Kolodny, expresses sympathy with Professor Anderson's focus on *social relations* of inequality in the workplace—"quasi-political relations of 'government' between employers and employees within the firm." But, he asks, what exactly "disquiets us" about these power relations and "what alternative social arrangements, even in principle . . . could put us at ease?"

Part of the problem, argues Kolodny, is that while economic enterprises often require managerial discretion, the resulting power over workers can be used for unjustified purposes that lack an economic rationale. And in addition, says Kolodny, we may still find it objectionable to be governed by the boss's discretion even when it is exercised only for justified purposes. But why? Is it that personal rule is always worse than the rule of general laws? Kolodny doubts that is the crux of the matter. Markets are unpredictable, and require flexibility, and laws, on the other hand, are made and administered by human beings. The basic difference, he suggests, between workplaces and political rule is that, in a democracy, governing is undertaken by delegates who are accountable to the citizens as equals: none is subordinate to others. Democratic citizens stand symmetrically with respect to one another in being governed and in having an equal opportunity to hold governors accountable. In the workplace, on the other hand, bosses may abuse their power and, even when they do not, they wield unaccountable power over workers, so workers are necessarily subordinate.

But, Kolodny asks in closing, how worrying is workplace subordination? Is it equivalent to political subordination? Three grounds suggest not. First, it is generally easier to leave a workplace than one's country; exit costs are lower. Second, we enjoy a greater degree of consent about where we work as compared with our country of membership. And, finally, workplace governance is ultimately subject to political rule, and so, "controlled from a standpoint of [democratic] equality." In the end, therefore, how troubled should we be that "our rights as employees are not like our rights as citizens?" Kolodny does not hazard an answer but underlines these questions' importance.

Finally, Tyler Cowen, an economist and a public commentator, advances a broad critique of Anderson's claims about the extent of worker domination in today's workplaces. He denies—on both theoretical and empirical grounds—the accuracy of describing private business firms as "communist dictatorships in our midst." He doubts that the costs of worker exit are as high as Anderson claims, and further doubts that individual firms enjoy much "monopsony" power over the workers they employ. He suspects, to the contrary, that because so many workers become attached to their particular workplaces—to their co-workers and various perks—that the bigger problem may be wage depression, rather than worker unfreedom. Even companies with monopsony power over workers seem often to cater to workers' "job quality preferences." Large firms in particular pay workers more and are generally protective of their workers' dignity and diversity: partly to guard the reputation of the company, but also to attract and retain talented workers.

Cowen further notes that when businesses do police "outside the workplace" activity, it is often to protect the dignity and *"the freedom of the other workers"* against, for example, racist or sexist Facebook posts. Indeed, he argues that co-workers and customers gain considerably from giving bosses discretion over firing, and while there are undoubtedly abuses, he doubts the abuses are widespread.

Cowen emphasizes, finally, that every governance arrangement involves trade-offs, and he worries that Anderson has not taken sufficient account of these in proposing alternatives to the current model. More broadly, he thinks Anderson exaggerates current managerial abuses in the workplace and discounts the extent to which today's capitalist workplaces are *"sources* of worker dignity, . . . freedoms, . . . pleasure and fulfillment."

In her wide-ranging reply, Anderson offers some clarifications of her thesis and a vigorous rejoinder to her critics.

In response to Hughes and Bromwich, she affirms that market society was harming some workers before the Industrial Revolution. Her main interest is the evolving "free market ideology" developed from the Levellers to Lincoln. She denies that those earlier free market thinkers, such as Adam Smith, can be understood as seeking to justify our commercial society. Anderson insists that "the Industrial Revolution decisively undermined the *model* early egalitarians promoted, of how a market society, *with appropriate reforms*, could liberate workers." And she observes, "The earlier thinkers are less to blame for vesting their hopes in an ideal that was destroyed by unforeseeable changes, than its current purveyors are for promulgating it in a world it does not remotely describe, either currently or in prospect."

In response to Kolodny, Anderson allows that hierarchical organization in the workplace is indispensible, but hierarchy does not justify the sort of arbitrary and unaccountable authority possessed by managers. Exercising autonomy in important aspects of one's life is, says Anderson, "a basic human need." Workers, she insists, should have a greater say in how their workplaces are organized even if "full workplace democracy" is infeasible.

Against Cowen, Anderson allows that, of course, the "costs and benefits of alternative workplace constitutions" must be assessed, but she insists that the abuse of worker freedoms is far more widespread than Cowen allows. Especially at the bottom of workplace hierarchies, among less skilled workers, abuses are rampant and include wage theft, unpredictable schedules, and sexual harassment, even while "academic research on labor is marginalized and underfunded." The fundamental problem, insists Anderson, is that "*the amount of respect, standing, and autonomy*" that workers "*get is roughly proportional to their market value.*" She insists against Cowen, in closing, that workers' exit rights are not sufficient to assure their basic "dignity and autonomy," they also need "voice" or "some share of autonomy in workplace decisions."

This impressive volume, and the insights and debates it contains, casts new light on power and justice in the workplace—questions important to the lives of nearly all, but far too rarely examined.

Author's Preface

Consider some facts about how employers today control their workers. Walmart prohibits employees from exchanging casual remarks while on duty, calling this "time theft."[1] Apple inspects the personal belongings of their retail workers, who lose up to a half-hour of unpaid time every day as they wait in line to be searched.[2] Tyson prevents its poultry workers from using the bathroom. Some have been forced to urinate on themselves, while their supervisors mock them.[3] About half of U.S. employees have been subject to suspicionless drug screening by their employers.[4] Millions are pressured by their employers to support particular political causes or candidates.[5]

If the U.S. government imposed such regulations on us, we would rightly protest that our constitutional rights were being violated. But American workers have no such rights against their bosses. Even speaking out against such constraints can get them fired. So most keep silent.

American public discourse is also mostly silent about the regulations employers impose on their workers. We have the language of fairness and distributive justice to talk about low wages and inadequate benefits. We know how to talk about the Fight for $15, whatever side of this issue we are on. But we don't have good ways to talk about the way bosses rule workers' lives.

Instead, we talk as if workers *aren't* ruled by their bosses. We are told that unregulated markets make us free, and that the only threat to our liberties is the state. We are told that in the market, all transactions are voluntary. We are told that, since workers freely enter and exit the labor contract, they are perfectly free under it: bosses have no more authority over workers than customers have over their grocer.

Labor movement activists have long argued that this is wrong. In ordinary markets, a vendor can sell their product to a buyer, and once the transaction is complete, each walks away as free from the other as before. Labor markets are different. When workers sell their labor to an employer, they have to hand *themselves* over to their boss, who then gets to order them around. The labor contract, instead of leaving the seller as free as before, puts the seller under the authority of their boss. Since the decline of the labor movement, however, we don't have effective ways to talk about this fact, and hence about what kinds of authority bosses should and shouldn't have over their workers.

These lectures aim to answer two questions. First, why do we talk as if workers are free at work, and that the only threats to individual liberty come from the state? Second, what would be a better way to talk about the ways employers constrain workers' lives, which can open up discussion about how the workplace could be designed to be more responsive to workers' interests?

My focus in both lectures is on *ideology*. An ideology is an abstract model that people use to represent and cope with the social world. Ideologies simplify the world, disregarding many of its features. An ideology is good if it helps us navigate it successfully. To help us, it must identify the normatively important features of the world, and the main causal connections between these features to which people can respond, enabling them to discover effective means to promoting their goals. Ideologies also help us orient our current evaluations of the world, highlighting what we think is already good or bad in it. Finally, they are vehicles for our hopes and dreams. A model may expose problems in our current world but also identify the causes of those problems such that, if those causes were removed or counteracted, we could achieve a better world. In other words, ideologies also function as *ideals*, offering us not only representations of the world as it is, but as it attractively *could be* if certain actions were undertaken.

I have so far explained what ideologies are in the nonpejorative sense of this term. We can hardly do without them. In personal experience, we have contact only with a small part of the world. To enable more comprehensive evaluation and planning, we need to represent aspects of the world that are not immediately experienced. And even the part that we do experience we filter through our ideologies to get a sense of what that experience means. We need to simplify to enable us to focus on the important things.

These facts about our cognitive limitations give rise to the danger that our models of the world may be ideological in the pejorative sense of this term. This occurs when our ideologies mask problematic features of our world, or cast those features in a misleadingly positive light, or lack the normative concepts needed to identify what is problematic about them, or misrepresent the space of possibilities so as to obscure better options, the means to realizing them, or their merits. Of course, no model can capture all normatively relevant features of the world. If it misses only relatively small, random, and idiosyncratic features, we should not condemn it. When these features are structurally embedded in the social world, so as to systematically undermine the interests of identifiable groups of people in serious or gratuitous ways, we need to revise our model to attend to them and identify means to change them. This is harder to do when the interests of those who dominate public discourse are already served by the dominant ideology.

Lecture 1 answers my first question—why we talk as if workers are free at work—by delving into the history of free market ideology. I argue that originally, many pro-market thinkers were sensitive to the liberty interests of workers, and had reasons to believe that free markets would help them, by liberating them from subordination to employers and other powerful organizations. They vested their hopes in a model that predicted that freeing up markets overall would reduce labor markets to minor features of a world in which most adults—at least if they were men—were self-employed. The Industrial Revolution destroyed those hopes, but not the idea of market society on which those hopes rested. The result is that we are working with a model of our world that omits the relations between employers and employees within which most of us work.

Lecture 2 corrects this omission by offering a way to understand and talk about what the employment relation is: it is a form of *government*, in which bosses govern workers. Most workplace governments in the United States are dictatorships, in which bosses govern in ways that are largely unaccountable to those who are governed. They don't merely govern workers; they *dominate* them. This is what I call *private government*. I offer this model as a critical tool to help us focus on important and problematic features of our world that affect the vital interests of workers, which the dominant ideology omits. I don't offer a blueprint for a better constitution of workplace government.

I offer a way of talking about the workplace, within which we can articulate how workers' interests are affected by the power employers wield over them, and how alternative constitutions of workplace government could be designed to be more responsive to their interests and more respectful of their dignity and autonomy.

I wish to thank Princeton University for inviting me to deliver the Tanner Lectures on Human Values in 2015, and the Tanner Lectures corporation for supporting my work. Don Herzog read the first draft of my lectures and provided very helpful comments that enabled me to polish my lectures for delivery. My commentators David Bromwich, Tyler Cowen, Ann Hughes, and Niko Kolodny, along with two anonymous reviewers for Princeton University Press, supplied splendid comments that enabled me to sharpen my ideas and clarify them for a broader readership. Alex Gourevitch, Stephen Macedo, and my editor, Rob Tempio, also made helpful suggestions. I thank them all for being such wonderful interlocutors.

Chapter 1

When the Market Was "Left"

Two Images of Market Society

The ideal of a free market society used to be a cause of the left. By "the left," I refer to egalitarian thinkers and participants in egalitarian social movements, starting with the Levellers in the mid-seventeenth century, continuing through the Enlightenment, the American and French Revolutions, and pre-Marxist radicals of the late eighteenth and early nineteenth centuries. In the United States, the association of market society with egalitarianism lasted through the Civil War.[1] We need to recover an understanding of why this was so, to better grasp the importance of evaluating ideals in their social context, and the problems with current ways of thinking about ideals of equality and freedom.

Consider two of the most famous passages ever written about market society. The first, by Adam Smith, sketches an image of market society as a free society of equals:

When an animal wants to obtain something either of a man or of another animal, it has no other means of persuasion but to gain the favour of those whose service it requires. A . . . spaniel endeavours by a thousand attractions to engage the attention of its master who is at dinner, when it wants to be fed by him. Man sometimes uses the same arts with his brethren, and . . . endeavours by every servile and fawning attention to obtain their good will. . . . But man has almost constant occasion for the help of his brethren, and it is in vain for him to expect it from their benevolence only. He will be more likely to prevail if he can interest their self-love in his favour, and shew them that it is for their own advantage to do for him what he requires of them. Whoever offers to another a bargain of any kind, proposes to do this. Give me that which I want, and you shall have this which you want, is the meaning of every such offer. . . . It is not from the benevolence of the butcher, the brewer, or the baker, that we expect our dinner, but from their regard to their own interest. We address ourselves, not to their humanity but to their self-love. . . . Nobody but a beggar chuses to depend chiefly upon the benevolence of his fellow-citizens.[2]

The second passage is by Karl Marx. He recasts Smith's image of the market as a mere portal into relations of domination and subordination:

[The] sphere . . . within whose boundaries the sale and purchase of labour-power goes on, is in fact a very Eden of the innate rights of man. There alone rule Freedom, Equality, Property and Bentham. Freedom, because both buyer and seller of a commodity, say of labour-power, are constrained only by their own free will. They contract as free agents, and the agreement they come to, is but the form in which they give legal expression to their common will. Equality, because each enters into relation with the other, as with a simple owner of commodities, and they exchange equivalent for equivalent. Property, because each disposes only of what is his own. And Bentham, because each looks only to himself....

On leaving this sphere of simple circulation or of exchange of commodities, which furnishes the "Free-trader Vulgaris" with his views and ideas, and with the standard by which he judges a society based on capital and wages, we think we can perceive a change in the physiognomy of our dramatis personae. He, who before was the money-owner, now strides in front as capitalist; the possessor of labour-power follows as his labourer. The one with an air of importance, smirking, intent on business; the other, timid and holding back, like one who is bringing his own hide to market and has nothing to expect but—a hiding.[3]

These two passages encapsulate a dramatic change in the egalitarian assessment of market society that took place between the eighteenth and nineteenth centuries. By *egalitarian*, I refer to an ideal of social relations. To be an egalitarian is to commend and promote a society in which its members interact as equals. This vague idea gets its shape by contrast with social hierarchy, the object of egalitarian critique. Consider three types or dimensions of social hierarchy: of authority, esteem, and standing. In a hierarchy of authority, occupants of higher rank get to order subordinates around. They exercise arbitrary and unaccountable power over their inferiors. In a hierarchy of esteem, occupants of higher rank despise those of inferior rank and extract tokens of deferential honor from them, such as bowing, scraping, and other rituals of self-abasement that inferiors display in recognition of the other's superiority. In a hierarchy of standing, the interests of those of higher rank *count* in the eyes of others, whereas the interests of inferiors do not: others are free to neglect them, and, in extreme cases, to trample upon them with impunity. Usually, these three hierarchies are joined.

Smith depicts market relations as egalitarian: the parties to exchange interact on terms of equal authority, esteem, and standing. He implies such egalitarian content by contrasting market exchange with begging, a kind of gift exchange in which subordinate parties offer tokens of asymmetrical esteem—"servile and fawning attention"—in return for something they want. The resort to servile fawning supposes that one's interests have negligible standing in the eyes of the other. The prospective benefactor may turn away a beggar just as a master may shoo away his spaniel from the dinner table. The transaction is humiliating to the beggar, and may involve his submission to the other's authority: servility is how servants behave toward their masters. Behind every gift exchange, ostensibly an altruistic affair, lurks dependency, contempt, and subordination.[4] By contrast, in market exchanges with the butcher, the brewer, and the baker, each party's interests have standing in the eyes of the other. Each party expresses this recognition by appealing to the other's interests as a reason for him to accept the exchange. The buyer is not an inferior, begging for a favor. Equally importantly, the buyer is not a superior who is entitled to simply order the butcher, the brewer, or the baker to hand over the fruits of his labor. Buyers must address themselves to the *other's* interests. *The parties each undertake the exchange with their dignity, their standing, and their personal independence affirmed by the other.* This is a model of social relations between free and equal persons.

Marx depicts this sunny egalitarian story of market exchange as utterly superficial. The market is a "noisy sphere, where everything takes place on the surface."[5] If this is Eden, it is just before the Fall. The action of real importance takes place once the contract is signed and the time comes to execute it. The worker is now dragged out of Eden into the sphere of production. His employer, like God, curses him to toil by the sweat of his brow. Now it is clear where the parties stand in the order of esteem: the capitalist enjoys an "air of importance," his employee is timid and cringing before him. They stand unequally in the order of authority: the capitalist strides in front, with the employee obligated to follow wherever his employer takes him. And they stand unequally in the order of standing: where the capitalist beams, in expectation of profit from the relationship, his worker "has nothing to expect but—a hiding." The performance of the contract embodies a profound asymmetry in whose interests *count*: henceforth, the worker will be required to toil under conditions that pay no regard to his interests, and every regard for the capitalist's profit.

What happened between Smith and Marx to reverse the egalitarian assessment of market society? It is not, as some have supposed, a revaluation of self-interest as a motive for relating to others. Smith *denies* Marx's claim that in market transactions "each looks only to himself." On his account, a successful bargain requires each to consider how they could bring some advantage *to the other*. Without a sympathetic appreciation for what might interest the other in transacting with oneself, and without acknowledging the independent standing of the other as someone whose property rights must be respected, no bargain will be struck.[6] Smith, no less than Marx, reviled selfishness as a basis for relating to others.[7]

What happened, I shall argue, was the Industrial Revolution. Smith wrote at the mere threshold of the Industrial Revolution, well before its implications for relations of production could be fully grasped. Marx wrote in its midst, at a point when workers were bearing its most frightful costs, and enjoying precious few of its benefits. The Industrial Revolution was a cataclysmic event for egalitarians, a fundamental turning point in egalitarian social thought.[8] It shattered their model of how a free society of equals might be built through market society. The history of egalitarianism in the nineteenth century is a history of extraordinary innovation and experimentation with alternative models, some of which rejected market society wholesale, others of which sought various revisions and supplements to it. Most of these experiments—utopian socialism, anarchism, syndicalism, Georgism, communism, democratic state socialism, workplace democracy, to name a few—either failed, were denied a real trial, or never managed to scale up. The most visible successes—notably, social democracy and labor unions—while still with us, are in decline or under stress in our postindustrial, globalized economy.

Intellectually, public discourse is underequipped to cope with these challenges. The Cold War induced a kind of amnesia over what the nineteenth-century struggles were about, presenting a radically reductionist picture of alternatives, especially in the United States. Images of free market society that made sense prior to the Industrial Revolution continue to circulate today as ideals, blind to the gross mismatch between the background social assumptions reigning in the seventeenth and eighteenth centuries, and today's institutional realities. We are told that our choice is between free markets and state control, when most adults live their working lives under a third thing entirely: *private government.*

My aim is to get a clearer view of what this third thing is, what challenges it poses to the ideal of a free society of equals, and how it might be reformed to enable that ideal to be realized under contemporary conditions. To gain clarity, we need to recover the intellectual context of egalitarian thought before the Industrial Revolution, when the market was "left."

Egalitarianism before the Industrial Revolution: Masterless Men, Levellers, and Locke

The Levellers undertook one of the first egalitarian social movements of the modern world. Arising in the English Civil War and strongly represented in Cromwell's New Model Army, they are best remembered for their calls for constitutional reform, including a nearly universal male franchise, parliamentary representation of districts in proportion to population, abolition of the House of Lords and the lords' privileges, and religious toleration.[9] Notwithstanding their name, given to them by Cromwell, who feared that democratization threatened a mass redistribution of property, the Levellers were also firm defenders of rights of private property and free trade. Captain John Clarke, in the Putney debates, affirmed that the law of nature establishes a right to property.[10] The Third Agreement of the People, promulgated by John Lilburne, William Walwyn, Thomas Prince, and Richard Overton, denied the state the power to "level mens Estates, destroy Propriety, or make all things Common"; to hinder freedom of foreign trade; to exempt anyone from paying their debts; or to enact permanent customs or excise taxes on goods, as these were "extreme burthensome and oppressive to Trade."[11] Lilburne attacked the state-granted monopolies of printing, preaching, and foreign trade as infringing on "the Common right of all the free-men of England" just as much as the recently barred monopolies of soap, salt, leather, and other goods.[12] He included, with full endorsement, the petition of William Sykes and Thomas Johnson against the licensed monopolies of the Eastland merchants, Merchant Adventurers, and other cartels in *Londons Liberty in Chains Discovered*.[13] Walwyn submitted a systematic argument for free trade to Whitehall.[14]

Given the tendencies of market society to generate inequality in income and wealth, what stake did this egalitarian movement see in promoting private property and free trade? To understand this, we must get beyond a narrow interpretation of egalitarianism in terms of current ideas about distributive justice.[15] Egalitarianism, more fundamentally, is about dismantling or taming social hierarchy. The Levellers' support for free trade formed an essential part of a larger program of liberating individuals from interlocking hierarchies of domination and subordination. They saw in free markets some essential institutional components of a free society of equals, based on their proliferation of opportunities for individuals to lead lives characterized by personal independence from the domination of others.

To see this, we must consider the social order against which the Levellers were rebelling. Early modern England was characterized by pervasive hierarchies of domination and subordination. Nearly all people but the king had superiors, who claimed nearly unaccountable discretionary authority to rule their lives. Lords governed their tenants and retainers, masters governed their servants, bishops their priests, priests their parishioners, captains their sailors, guilds their members, male heads of households their wives, children, and servants.

Government was everywhere, not just in the hands of the organizations we identify today with the modern state. The Anglican Church ran its own system of courts, censorship, and taxation. Church courts regularly excommunicated and fined parishioners for infractions of church regulations, even when that conduct was lawful. The church censored publications it regarded as heretical or blasphemous. It exacted tithes from parishioners, regardless of their religious beliefs.[16] Excommunication had consequences beyond expulsion from the church: by the Test Act, only those receiving Anglican Communion were eligible for public office. Guilds, too, operated their own court system, under which they routinely tried, fined, and jailed members who violated (or who merely refused to offer an oath that they had obeyed) the guild's minute regulations regarding matters such as the prices and quantities of goods for sale, and the location and days on which trading was permitted.[17] Under the common law of coverture, a wife's legal personhood was subsumed under her husband's: she could not own property, make contracts, sue or be sued in her own name. Her husband was legally entitled to all of her wages, to control her movements, and to inflict corporal punishment for disobedience. Divorce was very difficult to obtain.[18] Wives often acquired more leeway than the law recognized: mainly through contestation of their husbands' authority and appeal to custom, and rarely through prenuptial agreements and use of scattered laws and jurisdictions that limited coverture. Nevertheless, to speak of husbands' governing their wives was no mere metaphor.[19] In an era where production was not yet separated from the household, servants—that is, any employees under contract— lived under the government of their employers as subordinate members of an extended patriarchal family.[20] Apprentices were bound to service without pay. Under the common law of master and servant, regular employees had to work an entire year from sunup to sundown before acquiring entitlement to wages. Masters (employers) were free to withhold any amount of pay, without prorating, if their servants missed even a single day of work, or if they judged any part of their employees' work substandard. They were entitled to all of their servants' wages from moonlighting. Anti-enticement laws forbade competing employers to offer contracts to servants under contract to a different master.[21] Again, although custom and market conditions often gave servants more leeway than the law prescribed, they could not be considered free by today's standards.

Various ideologies rationalized these hierarchies.[22] One was the great chain of being. All creatures were linked in a great authoritarian chain of being reaching up to God, it was said, with everyone fixed to their particular link or social rank by birth. Everyone had some creature above and some below their place; even the king and pope were accountable to God; even the lowliest humans had dominion over animals. Breaking ranks would break the chain and unleash catastrophic disorder upon the world, detaching everyone from their connection to God.[23] Another was patriarchalism. The king, as father to his country, stood to his subjects as the father to all the members of his extended family—his wife, children, servants, and slaves. Just as the father enjoyed absolute dominion over the subordinate members of his household, and owned all its property, so the king enjoyed absolute authority over all his subjects, and owned all the land of the realm.[24] A third was the doctrine of original sin. Humanity's inherent proclivities toward sin justified comprehensive external constraint. Every sinner—every person—needed someone with authority over them to keep them in line.[25] Original sin rationalized absolute authority over others, and was the traditional justification for slavery.[26]

In sixteenth-century England, economic and religious changes began to set various individuals loose from traditional lines of authority, creating groups of "masterless men"—people who had no particular individual to whom they owed obedience.[27] The least advantaged were those displaced by agricultural developments, including enclosures and draining of the fens. Some went to London, seeking employment as casual laborers. Some became itinerant entertainers, traders, and cobblers. Some hung on in rural areas as cottagers and squatters in heaths, wastes, and forests, keeping a few animals, taking in knitting, and performing day labor. Some became vagabonds and beggars. Many of these individuals lived outside parishes or were otherwise unchurched. The more advantaged among masterless men were those who attained self-employment in a fixed establishment—yeoman farmers and long-term leaseholders, shopkeepers, artisans, and printers.

The rise of masterless men undermined the argument for authority based on the great chain of being.[28] That argument could explain why people fixed in a subordinate position should obey whoever was already bossing them around. But it could not identify any particular people to boss those unlinked from the chain of authority. Nor were many masterless men much interested in finding masters. They were making their livings on their own.

When Civil War broke out in the mid-seventeenth century, masterless men formed the core of Cromwell's New Model Army, which selected officers by ability rather than birth, and practiced open discussion among the ranks. Many men and officers were Levellers. Although the Levellers are mostly remembered for their constitutional demands to limit the authority of king, lords, and Parliament, and to make the state accountable to the people, their egalitarianism challenged other social hierarchies as well: the authority of the Church of England, and priests more generally, over parishioners; of men over women; of guilds and mercantile monopolies over artisans.

The Levellers arose in a time of religious ferment, the seeds of which had been laid in the Reformation. Martin Luther's doctrine of the priesthood of all believers was taken more literally by various Protestant sects than he intended. With the rise of printing and literacy among the people, laypersons began to read and think for themselves in theological matters. If believers enjoyed direct connection to God, unmediated by intervening links in the chain of being, then why grant authority to bishops or even to priests? The central religious conflict of the English Civil War was over church governance: the Puritans wanted to overthrow the Anglican bishops and universalize the Presbyterian system of governance by elders. Far more radically democratic sects arose during this period, such as Baptists, Quakers, Ranters, and Fifth Monarchists, featuring lay preachers. Leading Levellers came from dissenting sects. They demanded religious toleration, the abolition of tithes, church courts, and church censorship. Millennialism—the doctrine of Christ's imminent return to rule earth directly—was common among the sects. Christ's return implied his redemption of human beings from sin, and hence the demise of the doctrine of original sin and its support for authoritarianism. Individuals were thereby restored to their natural (prelapsarian) state of freedom and equality.[29]

Some dissenting sects drew feminist conclusions from their theologies. "The soul knows no difference of sex."[30] Women participated in church governance. Some became popular preachers. Divorce was liberalized, with men and women having equal rights to divorce their spouses. Quaker marriage vows omitted mention of a wife's duty to obey her husband. Margaret Fell, the wife of Quaker founder George Fox, had a prenuptial agreement denying Fox authority over her estate.[31] Leveller John Lilburne insisted that Adam and Eve, and hence all of their progeny, "were, by nature all equal and alike in power, dignity, authority, and majesty, none of them having by nature any authority, dominion, or magisterial power one over or above another." Turning the authoritarian doctrine of original sin on its head, he claimed that Adam's sin and that of all other men acting likewise consisted in the arrogant attempt to rule over anyone else without their consent.[32] Since, in the beginning, Adam had no one to rule over but Eve, the feminist implication of Lilburne's view is evident. Women such as Elizabeth Lilburne and Katherine Chidley were active in the Leveller movement. The *Petition of Women*, believed to be written by Chidley, insisted on the equal right of women to petition Parliament, and claimed for women "an interest in Christ equal unto men, as also of a proportionable share in the freedoms of this commonwealth."[33] Fifth Monarchists even advocated women's suffrage.[34]

In the context of patriarchalist justifications of state power, such feminist ideas served also to undermine monarchy. If husbands had no absolute dominion over their wives, then the king's claim to rule his subjects as the male head of household rules over everyone else in the family could not justify absolutism, or indeed much of any authority. If wives could hold title to property independently of their husbands, then the king's patriarchal claim to own all the property in the realm also came to naught.

In this era, support for private property and free trade went hand in hand with challenges to the monopoly of the Anglican Church over religious matters, as well as the king's patriarchalist claims to authority. The Root and Branch Petition of 1640, which called for the abolition of the episcopacy, complained of monopolies, patents, and tariffs, as well as the church's impositions of fines and excommunication for working and opening shop on holy days. Its persecution of dissenters drove clothiers to Holland, to the ruin of England's wool trade and of the poor workers who depended on that trade. The petition also railed against the church's control of the press, which was used to suppress dissenting religious tracts and to publish works claiming "that the subjects have no property in their estates, but that the king may take from them what he pleaseth."[35]

The Levellers' support for private property and free trade should be read in this context. The personal independence of masterless men and women in matters of thought and religion depended on their independence in matters of property and trade. If the king held title to all property, then subjects with land were reduced to mere copyholders, whose customary property rights could be extinguished by laws made without their participation, such as those calling for enclosures and expulsions of residents from fens.[36] If the church could fine dissenters in its own courts for violations of church decrees in restraint of trade, it would destroy their freedom of religion as well as their ways of making a living.

Monopolies were another form of state-licensed private government that threatened the personal independence of small traders and artisans. Whereas free trade promised economic growth, its principal advantage, from the Levellers' point of view, was its promotion of opportunities for economic independence. Abolition of guild monopolies would end the arbitrary and oppressive government of guilds over small merchants and artisans who did not care to obey the rules laid down by the larger ones.[37] (William Sykes, whose cause was championed by Lilburne, had been imprisoned in Rotterdam by England's Merchant Adventurers cartel, for refusing to swear an oath that he had obeyed all of their regulations concerning the cloth trade in Holland.[38]) This was not only a violation of rights to liberty. It was a violation of equality: "Patent societies swelling with a luciferian spirit, in desiring to advance into a higher room than their fellows, did by seruptitious Patents incorporate themselves," despite the fact that "every subject hath equall freedom with them" by the Magna Carta and other laws of England. Monopolies put the people "in a condition of vassalage," and reduce their hearts to "servility."[39]

Abolish the monopolies, and free trade would not merely liberate already existing small artisans from arbitrary private government. It would expand opportunities for many others to create their own businesses—to become self-employed, independent, masterless men. Charters of monopoly limited trade to particular towns. Abolish them, and trade, with its attendant opportunities for attaining independence, would spread across the entire country. Eliminate artificial barriers to trade, and "even servants" could risk investing in it, with the chance of gaining enough profit to become independent taxpayers.[40]

The Levellers did not neglect the benefits free trade would bring to those who would never attain self-employment. Abolition of monopolies would also strengthen the bargaining power of sailors, due to the multiplication of ships needed to bear a higher-volume foreign trade, and increase the purchasing power of "workmen of all sorts," by reducing prices.[41] The higher volume of trade would also employ many who were, under monopoly, unable to find work and thereby reduced to beggary.[42] As we have seen from Smith's observations, in the order of esteem and standing, earning one's living is better than begging. So free trade advances equality for many, even for those who do not enjoy full independence from the will of a master.

Thus, the Levellers rejected the principal arguments for social hierarchy of all kinds—the great chain of being, patriarchalism, original sin. Their critique of arbitrary and unaccountable state power was part and parcel of their critique of other forms of domination—of the church over all English subjects, of men over women, of lords over tenants, of guilds over artisans. The state underwrote these other forms of government by grants of monopoly (the established Church of England being just another kind of monopoly), restraints on free trade, and invasions of the birthrights of English subjects, which they saw as a form of property.[43] The Levellers supported property rights and free trade for the ways they secured and promoted the personal independence of individuals from the domination of others. These institutions promoted the ability of men and women to become masterless, and increased the dignity and bargaining power of those who remained servants, by raising their wages and real incomes and by lifting beggars from destitution to employment.

Locke, too, was an egalitarian who supported extensive rights to private property and contract. Did he link egalitarianism to rights to property and contract in the same ways as the Levellers? Lacking space for a more extensive commentary, I shall merely note some profound affinities between the Levellers and Locke, writing some decades after them. Locke's constitutional principles—popular sovereignty, a nearly universal male franchise, equality under the law, equal representation of districts, supremacy of the House of Commons—are all Leveller principles.[44] Like them, his egalitarian critique of arbitrary and unaccountable state power is deeply tied to his critique of other forms of government. In particular, his feminism (his insistence that wives are entitled to independent rights to property, freedom of contract, divorce, and personal autonomy from their husbands) is indispensable to his critique of patriarchalist defenses of absolute monarchy.[45] He also insists that property owners are not entitled to take advantage of the poor by conditioning an offer of subsistence on their submission to arbitrary power.[46] As with the Levellers, once we focus on the egalitarian interest in avoiding relations of domination and subjection, it is much easier to see how, in the context of seventeenth-century institutions, market society could be an egalitarian cause.

Egalitarianism before the Industrial Revolution: Smith

We have seen that in the seventeenth century, egalitarians supported private property and free trade because they anticipated that the growth of market society would help dismantle social hierarchies of domination and subordination. State-licensed monopolies were instruments by which the higher ranks oppressively governed the middling and lower ranks. Opposition to economic monopolies was part of a broader agenda of dismantling monopolies across all domains of social life: not just the guilds, but monopolies of church and press, monopolization of the vote by the rich, and monopolization of family power by men. Eliminate monopoly, and far more people would be able to attain personal independence and become masterless men and women. Even those who remained servants would gain esteem and standing through enhanced income and bargaining power with respect to their masters.

Did that vision continue through the eighteenth century? We need only consult the leading eighteenth-century advocate of market society, Adam Smith, to know the answer. Today, Smith is read as advocating market society because it would lead to economic growth and an efficient allocation of resources. These are unquestionably significant themes in his writings. However, he did not think that economic growth and efficiency were the leading virtues of market society. Rather, the transition from feudalism to market society, driven by the rise of commerce and manufactures, led to "order and good government, and with them the liberty and security of individuals . . . who had before lived almost in a continual state of war with their neighbours, and of servile dependency upon their superiors. This . . . is *by far the most important of all their effects.*"[47]

The critical mediating factor leading to these favorable effects was the transition from gift to market exchange as the principal basis by which individuals satisfied their needs. Feudalism was based on "hospitality": because markets were undeveloped, the landlord could spend his surplus

> in no other way than by maintaining a hundred or a thousand men. He is at all times, therefore, surrounded with a multitude of retainers and dependants, who, having no equivalent to give in return for their maintenance, but being fed entirely by his bounty, must obey him. . . . The occupiers of land were in every respect as dependent upon the great proprietor as his retainers. Even such of them as were not in a state of villanage, were tenants at will. . . . A tenant at will . . . is as dependent upon the proprietor as any servant or retainer whatever, and must obey him with as little reserve. . . . The subsistence of both is derived from his bounty, and its continuance depends upon his good pleasure. Upon the authority which the great proprietors necessarily had . . . over their tenants and retainers, was founded the power of the ancient barons. They necessarily became the judges in peace, and the leaders in war, of all who dwelt upon their estates. . . . Not only the highest jurisdictions, both civil and criminal, but the power of levying troops, of coining money, and even that of making bye-laws for the government of their own people, were all rights possessed allodially by the great proprietors of land.[48]

To depend on the good will of another for one's subsistence puts one at the mercy of the other, and under his subjection. Gifts are not free: "hospitality" is given in return for obedience. The result is *private government*: the gift-giver's unaccountable dominion over the recipients of his good will. But private government was *bad* government. Not only did it reduce most people to a state of "servile dependency," but also the feudal lords were always at war with one another, leaving the country "a scene of violence, rapine, and disorder."[49]

The rise of commerce and manufacturing had ironically beneficial results:

> All for ourselves, and nothing for other people, seems, in every age of the world, to have been the vile maxim of the masters of mankind. As soon, therefore, as they could find a method of consuming the whole value of their rents themselves, they had no disposition to share them with any other persons. For a pair of diamond buckles, perhaps, or for something as frivolous and useless, they exchanged the maintenance, or, what is the same thing, the price of the maintenance of 1000 men for a year, and with it the whole weight and authority which it could give them . . . thus, for the gratification of the most childish, the meanest, and the most sordid of all vanities they gradually bartered their whole power and authority.[50]

On Smith's account, the rise of commerce and manufacturing led people to leave the lords' estates to become artisans and tradesmen. Although the latter still depended on the great proprietors' expenditures for a living, now any given lord contributed only a small proportion of the subsistence of any of them. Hence no lord was in a position to command any of them: he got only buckles, not authority, for his payment. The substitution of market exchange for gift exchange thereby liberated artisans and tradesmen from "servile dependency." A similar process liberated the farmers. As the lords dismissed their retainers, they did not need to take so much of the harvest for the maintenance of hundreds or thousands. So the lords also dismissed many tenants at will, while raising rents on the remainder. The latter were willing to pay higher rents only in return for long-term leases. By this means, the farmers were also liberated from servility to the lords. Tenants at will, fearful of eviction if they do not obey every whim of their landlord, must bow and scrape before them. Farmers protected by long-term leases need only pay the rent. The market nexus replaces a relation of domination and subjection with an arm's-length exchange on the basis of mutual interest and personal independence. By undermining the authority of the landlords, market society also increased the power of the national government, which brought peace, order, and the rule of law.[51]

So far, Smith's account of the rise of market society is historical. It does not take into account the *expected* effects of setting markets *free*—of removing all monopolizing constraints on trade. Chief among these constraints were primogeniture and entails, which kept nearly all land locked up and undivided in the possession of the firstborn sons of a few great families. Smith condemned these constraints as "founded upon the most absurd of all suppositions, . . . that every successive generation of men have not an equal right to the earth," but that land ownership be restrained by "the fancy of those who died perhaps five hundred years ago."[52] This arrangement was inefficient, because great landowners are more interested in conspicuous consumption than improving the land, which requires laborious attention "to small savings and small gains."[53] The most efficient agricultural producers are the yeoman farmers, small proprietors who work their own land. Neither sharecroppers nor tenants at will nor even leaseholders had a great incentive to invest in land improvements, because their landlord would appropriate part or all of the gains. Nor was slavery efficient, because slaves have no incentive to work hard.[54] If primogeniture and entail were abolished, great estates would be divided upon the death of the owner and sold. Land prices would fall because a greater supply of land would reach the market. This would put farms within reach of the most productive—the yeoman farmers. Smith looked to North America as a model of what would happen: even individuals of very modest means could buy their own farms, and yeoman farmers dominated the agricultural sector.[55]

Smith believed that in a fully free market, the commercial and manufacturing sectors would similarly be dominated by small-scale enterprises, run by independent artisans and merchants, with at most a few employees. Large-scale enterprises were a product of state-licensed monopolies, tariffs, and other mercantilist protections. It was only necessary to raise the large concentrations of capital used by joint-stock corporations for four types of "routine" business that required no innovation or entrepreneurial vision: banking, insurance, canals, and water utilities. With or without special state protections, they would tend to fail.[56] In a free market, with barriers to entry eliminated, firms managed by their owners would out-compete the directors of joint-stock corporations because the former, risking their own money, would invest more energy, attention, and skill in their businesses. With many entrants into the open market, rates of profit would fall. When profits are low, few great fortunes can be accumulated, so nearly all capital owners will have to work for a living.[57]

No wonder Smith's pin factory, his model of an enterprise with an efficient division of labor, employed only ten workers.[58] *The Wealth of Nations* was published in 1776. Smith was writing only at the threshold of the Industrial Revolution. The spinning jenny had been invented in 1764, kept secret until it was patented in 1770, and was only beginning to be used in a few factories by 1776. No one could have anticipated the rise of Blake's "dark, satanic mills" on the basis of such slender evidence. Smith reasonably believed that economies of scale were negligible for the production of most goods.

Thus we see that Smith's economic vision of a free market society aligns with the Levellers' vision more than a century earlier. Abolish guilds, monopolies, tariffs, restrictions on land sales, and other state-enforced restrictions on "natural liberty," and concentrations of great wealth would be dissipated, while labor would enjoy a "liberal reward."[59] Any remaining inequalities of wealth would hardly matter. In Smith's day, there were only two things great wealth could buy that were beyond the reach of those of modest means: dominion over others, and vanities.[60] For the rich, the rise of market society replaced the pursuit of dominion with the pursuit of trifling vanities. This was a huge win from an egalitarian point of view. Eliminate barriers to free markets, and the fortunes of the rich would be quickly dissipated, while opportunities for self-employment would proliferate.[61] This would be another huge advance for equality. It is a deeply humane vision.

Egalitarianism before the Industrial Revolution: From Paine to Lincoln

Imagine a free market economy in which nearly everyone either is self-employed as a yeoman farmer, artisan, or small merchant or else is a worker in a small firm with high and rising wages, sufficient to enable enough saving so that one could purchase one's own farm or workshop after a few years. Markets would be perfectly competitive, so no one would enjoy market power over others. Profits would be low and everyone would have to work for a living, so labor would not be despised. Material inequality would be limited to individual differences in personal labor effort and skill, not to inequalities in birth, state-granted privileges, capital ownership, or command over others' labor. Everyone would meet on an equal footing with everyone else. All would enjoy personal independence. No one would be subject to another's domination. Would this not be close to an egalitarian utopia, a truly free society of equals?

Egalitarians thought they saw such a utopia emerging in America. This is hard to imagine today, given that the United States is by far the most unequal among the rich countries of the world. Yet from Smith's day to Lincoln's, America was the leading hope of egalitarians on both sides of the Atlantic.

To be sure, slavery was a monstrous blot on that hope.[62] But in the heady years of the American Revolution and the early American republic, optimism reigned. The Northwest Ordinance of 1787 had prohibited the spread of slavery to the northwestern territories. By 1804, all the Northern states had passed laws to abolish slavery. Many thought that slavery was headed for a natural death as an inefficient form of production, as Smith had argued.

In the age of revolutions, America offered opportunities to free workers unlike any other country in the world. The great majority of the free population was self-employed, either as a yeoman farmer or an independent artisan or merchant. Journeymen had a good chance of owning their own enterprise after a few years. In the North, not only slavery, but other forms of unfree labor, such as apprenticeship and indentured service, were in steep decline.[63] The future appeared to promise real personal independence for all.

Thomas Paine was the great advocate of this vision in the revolutionary era, in three countries. Raised as a Quaker and apprenticed as a stay maker, Paine despised social hierarchy and dedicated his life to political agitation for equality. He was a hero of the American Revolution for writing *Common Sense*, the most popular and influential political pamphlet up to that time. *Common Sense* rallied the colonists not simply around independence, but around the idea that America, as a republic, would show the world how a free society of equals would look. During the French Revolution, he was elected to the National Convention. He was also lionized by American and English labor radicals, who read his writings well into the nineteenth century. The Chartists, active from 1838 to 1848, put him on their reading list.

Paine's economic views were broadly libertarian. Individuals can solve nearly all of their problems on their own, without the state meddling in their affairs.[64] All improvements in productive technology are due to enterprising individuals, who hope that government will just leave them alone.[65] A good government does nothing more than secure individuals in "peace and safety" in the free pursuit of their occupations, enjoying the fruits of their labors, with the lowest possible tax burden.[66] Paine was a lifelong advocate of commerce, free trade, and free markets.[67] He argued against state regulation of wages, claiming that workers should bargain over wages on the free market.[68] Against populist suspicion of finance, Paine was a leading advocate of chartering the Bank of North America, in part to supply credit for artisans, in part as a defense against the state's issuing too much paper money.[69]

Most problems, he argued, are the result of government. Excess printing of paper money (not hoarding, as popular crowds supposed) was the cause of inflation. So he criticized demands for price controls during the Revolutionary War inflation, and argued against price controls at the French National Convention.[70] He called for hard money and fiscal responsibility.[71] In most states—England was his chief example—government is the principal burden on society, waging war, inflating the debt, and imposing burdensome taxes. Government spending is mostly wasteful. Taxation is theft; government is a "system of war and extortion."[72] People living off government pay are social parasites, oppressing the industrious.[73] Government is also the chief cause of poverty, due to "the greedy hand of government thrusting itself into every corner and crevice of industry, and grasping the spoil of the multitude."[74] He proposed a plan to eliminate poverty in England by rebating the oppressive taxes the poor were forced to pay. Cut taxes drastically, and the poor will do fine, while the better off will no longer have to pay poor rates to support the welfare system.[75]

Paine's views on political economy sound as if they could have been ripped out of today's establishment Republican Party playbook.[76] How, given these positions, could he have been the hero of labor radicals in the United States and England for decades after his death in 1809? He shows enormous faith in free markets and does not display a trace of the anti-capitalist class conflict that characterized nineteenth-century politics. The answer is that labor radicals saw access to self-employment as central to avoiding poverty and attaining standing as equals in society. In the late eighteenth and early nineteenth centuries, the most radical workers were not the emerging industrial proletariat, but artisans who operated their own enterprises.[77] As such, they were simultaneously capitalists and workers: they owned their own capital, but also had to work for a living. As operators of small businesses, they favored commerce and open access to markets and credit. America, with nearly universal self-employment either actually realized or a seemingly realistic prospect for free workers, offered proof of concept. Paine was the greatest popularizer of the American experiment.

In an economic context in which the self-employed find their status and opportunities threatened by powerful institutions, it does not make sense to pit workers against capitalists. Popular politics instead pits the common working people against elites—that is, whoever controls the more powerful institutions. It may also pit the common working people against idlers—those who, like aristocrats, do not have to work for a living, but live off the labor of others. The Levellers saw the state as underwriting all kinds of oppressive private governments— of landlords, the established church, guilds, patriarchy. In Paine, however, the pre-industrial egalitarian vision narrowed to focus on the state. Nearly all states, other than the United States, were corrupt. Corruption exists whenever the state favors elites at the expense of ordinary working people—when it acts "by partialities of favor and oppression."[78] Paine enumerated several forms of unjust favoritism that oppressed ordinary working people. Idle landlords received special representation in the House of Lords, and a separate set of laws applicable only to them.[79] The state gave charters (monopolies) to elites, at the expense of the right of all people to engage in trade, and at the cost of economic growth.[80] It taxed working people to lavishly fund the king and his court of idlers.[81] It handed out sinecures to buy the votes of members of Parliament, and provide places for the worthless younger sons of aristocrats who, under primogeniture, would receive no inheritance.[82] The worst corruption by far was the state's waging of bloody and colossally expensive wars to support plunder and imperialism, at the cost of exploding tax burdens and public debt. Because the aristocracy controlled the system of taxation, they exempted themselves from most taxes and placed the burdens of funding these wars on working people, through oppressive sales taxes.[83]

Paine's low-tax, free-trade libertarian agenda made considerable sense for an export-led agricultural economy facing high grain prices, as was true for late eighteenth-century America. "The commerce by which [America] hath enriched herself are the necessaries of life, and will always have a market while eating is the custom of Europe."[84] Free market wages were high in a country suffering from chronic labor shortages, and in which self-employment was a ready option for nearly all.[85] When the bulk of the population is self-employed, pleading for relief from state meddling is quite a different proposition than it would be today. There is not much call for employment regulations if there are few employees, and virtually all have a ready exit into self-employment. When no enterprises are large enough to have market power, there is no need for anti-trust regulation. When land is abundant and practically free, land use and pollution regulations are hardly needed because people are spread out and environmental effects (as far as people understood at the time) minimal. When people can appraise the quality of virtually all goods for sale on inspection, and nearly everyone grows what they eat, there is little need for laws regulating the safety of consumer goods. Arcane financial instruments could not bring an economy to its knees in an era in which banking was primitive and much of the economy was not monetized. So there was little need for complex financial regulation. In the absence of any notion of central banking or modern monetary policy, the gold standard was a better policy than one allowing states to issue paper money at will—a practice that led to destructive inflation in Paine's day. Paine's America probably came as close as anywhere in the world to avoiding market failures, as contemporary economists define them.

One issue, however, continued to bother Paine near the end of his life: widespread poverty. In *The Rights of Man*, he argued that poverty in England could be solved by rebating the taxes the poor paid to support England's king, court, sinecures, military, and colonial system. Roll back this wasteful spending, end the poor rates, and there would still be a surplus that could be rebated to the poor or spent on educating their children, which would prevent their falling into poverty as adults.

Implicit in his thinking was a more systematic appreciation of the causes of poverty. It could not be simply due to a corrupt state oppressing the poor with excessive taxes to fund wasteful spending, or to monopolizing and other forms of state favoritism. People needed access to education to avoid poverty. In "Agrarian Justice," Paine went much further in questioning the adequacy even of the system of nearly universal self-employment that he saw in America. The great defect of such a system is that it makes families depend on labor to avoid poverty. What happens when, due to old age, disability, illness, or death, there is no one in the family able to work? The rich had a stock of capital on which they could live without working. To prevent poverty, everyone would need something comparable. Paine proposed a system of universal social insurance, including old-age pensions, survivor benefits, and disability payments for families whose members could not work. In addition, he proposed a system of universal stakeholder grants for young adults starting out in life, which they could use to obtain further education or tools, so their labor would earn enough to avoid poverty. This was the first realistic comprehensive social insurance proposal in the world, and the first realistic proposal to end poverty.

Paine insisted that this did not represent an abandonment of his principles of private property and free markets. Individualist to the last, Paine justified his social insurance system on strict Lockean property principles. Revenues for social insurance would come from an inheritance tax, which in his day amounted to a land tax. This was just, because landowners, in enclosing a part of the earth that was originally held in common by all, had failed to compensate everyone else for their taking. Even if they had mixed their labor with the land in the original appropriation, this entitled them only to the value their labor added to the land. They could not claim to deserve the value of the raw natural resources, or the value of surrounding uses that enhanced the market price of land. Each member of society was entitled to their per capita share of these values. So, landowners still owed a rent to everyone else. By this reasoning, Paine justified social insurance as a universal right, not a charity.[86]

This emergence of a systematic economic account of poverty, not tied to corrupt special favors dealt out by the state, was to remain underdeveloped in Painite radical labor ideology. English radicals such as William Cobbett and the Chartists continued to focus on political corruption as the source of the independent worker's oppression. The idea of social insurance as a systematic solution to a problem inherent in a system that let free markets be the sole mechanism for allocating income had to await the rise of socialism before it was taken up again—and then, ironically, by socialism's enemies. Bismarck, the notorious anti-socialist who banned the activities of the German Social Democratic Party, implemented the first social insurance program in the world.

Even as the Industrial Revolution was bringing the presocialist era of egalitarian labor radicalism to an end in Europe—Chartism breathed its last gasp in 1848—the dream of a free society of equals built on independent small producers continued in the United States through the Civil War. This was the ideal on which the antebellum Republican Party was founded. Its central principle, anti-slavery, was based not so much on the moral wrong slavery inflicted on the slaves (although this was acknowledged), as it was on the threat slavery posed to the self-employed worker. The central platform of the antebellum Republican Party was to prohibit the extension of slavery in the territories. The creation of gigantic slave plantations in the territories would absorb land that would otherwise be available for free men to make it on their own as yeoman farmers, and consign them to wage labor for the rest of their lives.[87] President Lincoln articulated the view of his party. He rejected the theory that all workers must either be wage workers or slaves—either hired or bought by capital—and, if hired, "fixed in that condition for life." This he condemned as the "mud-sill" theory of society—the idea, advanced by proslavery Senator James Hammond of South Carolina, that every society needed an inferior class of people consigned to drudgery, on which to base civilization, just as every soundly built house needs to rest on a mudsill.[88] Lincoln advanced a rival view

> that there is not, of necessity, any such thing as the free hired laborer being fixed to that condition for life.... Many independent men in this assembly doubtless a few years ago were hired laborers. And their case is almost, if not quite, the general rule. The prudent, penniless beginner in the world labors for wages awhile, saves a surplus with which to buy tools or land for himself, then labors on his own account another while, and at length hires another new beginner to help him. This, say its advocates, is free labor—the just, and generous, and prosperous system, which opens the way for

all, gives hope to all, and energy, and progress, and improvement of condition to all.[89]

This progress of free labor to full self-employment is what the "society of equals" was all about.[90]

Was the Republican promise truly "for all"? The Homestead Act of 1862 was an attempt to fulfill that promise. However, to masses of wage laborers in the big Northern cities, this was already an unrealistic dream that did not speak to their needs as workers. It was even more unrealistic for free blacks, Chinese indentured servants, Mexican-American peons, and American Indians, who occupied "halfway houses of semi-free labor."[91] The Thirteenth Amendment, which abolished slavery, attempted to advance that promise for nonwhites. Under it, peonage and other forms of involuntary servitude were prohibited—although litigation against various forms of peonage continued well into the 1940s, long after the dream of universal self-employment was dashed forever. More revealing for our purposes is the fact that the Thirteenth Amendment was the basis for the Civil Rights Act of 1866, which banned racial discrimination in the sale and rental of property. That a law banning slavery supported a right to buy land made sense only given a background ideology that identified free labor with self-employment, which required that the worker could buy or rent his capital. Yet that promise was left unfulfilled by the failure of the radical Republican's vision of Reconstruction, which would have divided the former slave plantations among the freed people.

Even had the radical Republican program of Reconstruction been enacted, its ideal of free labor was doomed. What began as a hopeful, inspiring egalitarian ideal in the United States self-destructed in three ways.

First, the ideal of universal self-employment never managed to incorporate the unpaid domestic labor essential to family life, which was performed overwhelmingly by women. Congressional debate over the Thirteenth Amendment made it clear that women were excluded from the promise of fully free labor. Notwithstanding the amendment, husbands retained property in their wives' labor.[92] This was a contradiction inherent in the free labor ideal, as the independence of men depended on their command over their wives' labor.[93] Hidden in the ostensible universalism and hyperindividualism of the ideal was a presumption of male governance over their wives'—and children's—labor. The feminist movement, which arose from the abolitionist movement, was to highlight this contradiction, as women came to demand independent and equal standing in the workplace and at home.

Second, the Civil War, which ended slavery in the name of independent labor, ironically propelled the very forces that put the universalization of that ideal further out of reach, even for the class of white men. It was a powerful driver of industrialization, and hence of the triumph of large enterprises using the wage labor system over the small proprietor.

Third, the ideal contained an implicit esteem hierarchy that was ultimately to turn its egalitarian aspirations upside down. If the only fully respectable labor is independent, self-employed labor, if the way to attain recognition as an equal is to operate one's own enterprise, then what is one to make of those who remain wage laborers for their whole lives? Lincoln was clear: "If any continue through life in the condition of the hired laborer, it is not the fault of the system, but because of either a dependent nature which prefers it, or improvidence, folly, or singular misfortune."[94] Even in 1861, with the frontier still open, the burgeoning pace of immigration and urban industrialization was outrunning the flow of men out West. Lincoln's disparaging judgment of wage laborers is akin to blaming those left standing in a game of musical chairs, while denying that the structure of the game has anything to do with the outcome. Thus, what began as an egalitarian ideal ended as another basis for esteem hierarchy: to raise the businessman on a higher plane than the wage worker.[95]

The Cataclysm of the Industrial Revolution

The Industrial Revolution shattered the egalitarian ideal of universal self-government in the realm of production. Economies of scale overwhelmed the economy of small proprietors, replacing them with large enterprises that employed many workers. Opportunities for self-employment shrank dramatically in the course of the nineteenth century, and have continued to shrink to the present day. The Industrial Revolution also altered the nature of work and the relations between owners and workers in manufacturing, widening the gulf between the two.

There was a hierarchy of masters over journeymen and apprentices in the small-scale preindustrial workshop. Apprentices, in particular, without the right to a wage (like many American interns today), were unfree. Yet several factors constrained this hierarchy. Masters worked side by side with journeymen, performing the same labor while teaching apprentices the same skills. The fact that they performed work of the same kind as their subordinates, in the same workshop, softened the conditions of work. Masters could not make their subordinates labor in a shop whose conditions were so uncomfortable or unsafe that they would be unwilling to work there themselves. Nor could they impose a pace of work more relentless than they would be personally willing to endure. The pace of the typical artisanal workshop was relaxed, and included many breaks. Masters fraternized with their journeymen. Alcohol passed freely between masters and journeymen even during working hours. Finally, in the United States through the early years of the nineteenth century, skilled journeymen enjoyed a reasonable expectation of being able to set up shop for themselves after a few years of wage labor, in the manner Lincoln thought was the norm. With such a short, easy bridge from one rank to the next, it was relatively easy for workers to reconcile the hierarchy that did exist with egalitarian republican values.[96]

The Industrial Revolution dramatically widened the gulf between employers and employees in manufacturing. Employers no longer did the same kind of work as employees, if they worked at all. Mental labor was separated from manual labor, which was radically deskilled. Ranks within the firm multiplied. Leading executives might not even work in the same building. This facilitated a severe degradation of working conditions. Workers were subject to the relentless, grueling discipline of the clock and the machine. Employers, instead of drinking with their workers, preached temperance, industry, punctuality, and discipline. Conditions were harsh, hours long, wages low, and prospects for advancement, regardless of how hard one worked, minimal.

The nineteenth century saw the spread of total institutions across society: the prison, the asylum, the hospital, the orphanage, the poorhouse, the factory. Jeremy Bentham's notorious prison plan, the Panopticon, was his model for these other institutions.[97] Other liberals, such as Joseph Priestley, allied with factory owners and social reformers to promote these new types of hyperdisciplinary institution. Here lay the central contradiction of the new liberal order: "Though these radicals preached independence, freedom, and autonomy in polity and market, they preached order, routine, and subordination in factory, school, poorhouse, and prison."[98]

Preindustrial labor radicals, viewing the vast degradation of autonomy, esteem, and standing entailed by the new productive order in comparison with artisan status, called it *wage slavery*. Liberals called it *free labor*. The difference in perspective lay at the very point Marx highlighted. If one looks only at the conditions of entry into the labor contract and exit out of it, workers appear to meet their employers on terms of freedom and equality. That was what the liberal view stressed. But if one looks at the actual conditions experienced in the workers' fulfilling the contract, the workers stand in a relation of profound subordination to their employer. That was what the labor radicals stressed.

In this light, let us now return to the contrast between Smith and Marx with which this lecture opened. It is often supposed that their differing assessments of market society were based on fundamentally opposed values. Yet both marveled at the ways market society drove innovation, productive efficiency, and economic growth. And both deplored the deskilling and stupefying effects of an increasingly fine-grained division of labor on workers.[99] They differed rather on what they expected market society to offer to workers. Smith's greatest hope—the hope shared by labor radicals from the Levellers to the Chartists, from Paine to Lincoln—was that freeing up markets would dramatically expand the ranks of the self-employed, who would exercise talent and judgment in governing their own productive activities, independent of micromanaging bosses. No wonder Smith's optimistic representation of market relations focused on the butcher, the brewer, and the baker—all independent proprietors. Free market society could be championed as "left," as an egalitarian cause, so long as "by far the most important" of its effects was "the liberty . . . of individuals . . . who had before lived almost in a continual state of . . . servile dependency upon their superiors." With the Industrial Revolution, the pervasiveness of markets in *labor* returned manufacturing workers to an even deeper state of subjection to their superiors than before. Smith, who despised selfishness, disparaged the quest to accumulate vast fortunes, and cited "the disposition to admire, and almost to worship, the rich and the powerful . . . [as] the great and most universal cause of the corruption of our moral sentiments" would not have approved.[100]

Preindustrial egalitarians had no answer for the challenges of the Industrial Revolution. Their model of how to bring about a free society of equals through free markets via near-universal self-employment was shattered. Advocates of laissez faire, who blithely applied the earlier arguments for market society to a social context that brought about the very opposite of the effects that were predicted and celebrated by their predecessors, failed to recognize that the older arguments no longer applied. Thus arose a symbiotic relationship between libertarianism and authoritarianism that blights our political discourse to this day. For what we have yet to adequately grasp is the nature of the challenge before us: *private government*.

Chapter 2

Private Government

Communist Dictatorships in Our Midst

Imagine a government that assigns almost everyone a superior whom they must obey. Although superiors give most inferiors a routine to follow, there is no rule of law. Orders may be arbitrary and can change at any time, without prior notice or opportunity to appeal. Superiors are unaccountable to those they order around. They are neither elected nor removable by their inferiors. Inferiors have no right to complain in court about how they are being treated, except in a few narrowly defined cases. They also have no right to be consulted about the orders they are given.

There are multiple ranks in the society ruled by this government. The content of the orders people receive varies, depending on their rank. Higher-ranked individuals may be granted considerable freedom in deciding how to carry out their orders, and may issue some orders to some inferiors. The most highly ranked individual takes no orders but issues many. The lowest-ranked may have their bodily movements and speech minutely regulated for most of the day.

This government does not recognize a personal or private sphere of autonomy free from sanction. It may prescribe a dress code and forbid certain hairstyles. Everyone lives under surveillance, to ensure that they are complying with orders. Superiors may snoop into inferiors' e-mail and record their phone conversations. Suspicionless searches of their bodies and personal effects may be routine. They can be ordered to submit to medical testing. The government may dictate the language spoken and forbid communication in any other language. It may forbid certain topics of discussion. People can be sanctioned for their consensual sexual activity or for their choice of spouse or life partner. They can be sanctioned for their political activity and required to engage in political activity they do not agree with.

The economic system of the society run by this government is communist. The government owns all the nonlabor means of production in the society it governs. It organizes production by means of central planning. The form of the government is a dictatorship. In some cases, the dictator is appointed by an oligarchy. In other cases, the dictator is self-appointed.

Although the control that this government exercises over its members is pervasive, its sanctioning powers are limited. It cannot execute or imprison anyone for violating orders. It can demote people to lower ranks. The most common sanction is exile. Individuals are also free to emigrate, although if they do, there is usually no going back. Exile or emigration can have severe collateral consequences. The vast majority have no realistic option but to try to immigrate to another communist dictatorship, although there are many to choose from. A few manage to escape into anarchic hinterlands, or set up their own dictatorships.

This government mostly secures compliance with carrots. Because it controls all the income in the society, it pays more to people who follow orders particularly well and promotes them to higher rank. Because it controls communication, it also has a propaganda apparatus that often persuades many to support the regime. This need not amount to brainwashing. In many cases, people willingly support the regime and comply with its orders because they identify with and profit from it. Others support the regime because, although they are subordinate to some superior, they get to exercise dominion over inferiors. It should not be surprising that support for the regime for these reasons tends to increase, the more highly ranked a person is.

Would people subject to such a government be free? I expect that most people in the United States would think not. Yet most work under just such a government: it is the modern workplace, as it exists for most establishments in the United States. The dictator is the chief executive officer (CEO), superiors are managers, subordinates are workers. The oligarchy that appoints the CEO exists for publicly owned corporations: it is the board of directors. The punishment of exile is being fired. The economic system of the modern workplace is communist, because the government—that is, the establishment—owns all the assets,[1] and the top of the establishment hierarchy designs the production plan, which subordinates execute. There are no internal markets in the modern workplace. Indeed, the boundary of the firm is *defined* as the point at which markets end and authoritarian centralized planning and direction begin.[2]

Most workers in the United States are governed by communist dictatorships in their work lives. Usually, those dictatorships have the legal authority to regulate workers' off-hour lives as well—their political activities, speech, choice of sexual partner, use of recreational drugs, alcohol, smoking, and exercise. Because most employers exercise this off-hours authority irregularly, arbitrarily, and without warning, most workers are unaware of how sweeping it is. Most believe, for example, that their boss cannot fire them for their off-hours Facebook postings, or for supporting a political candidate their boss opposes. Yet only about half of U.S. workers enjoy even partial protection of their off-duty speech from employer meddling.[3] Far fewer enjoy legal protection of their speech on the job, except in narrowly defined circumstances. Even where they are entitled to legal protection, as in speech promoting union activity, their legal rights are often a virtual dead letter due to lax enforcement: employers determined to keep out unions immediately fire any workers who dare mention them, and the costs of litigation make it impossible for workers to hold them accountable for this.

I expect that this description of communist dictatorships in our midst, pervasively governing our lives, often to a far greater degree of control than the state, would be deeply surprising to most people. Certainly many U.S. CEOs, who think of themselves as libertarian individualists, would be surprised to see themselves depicted as dictators of little communist governments. Why do we not recognize such a pervasive part of our social landscape for what it is? Should we not subject these forms of government to at least as much critical scrutiny as we pay to the democratic state? My project in this lecture is to explain why public discourse and political philosophy largely neglect the pervasiveness of authoritarian governance in our work and off-hours lives and why we should return our attention to it, and to sketch some thoughts as to what we should do about it—for neglect of these issues is relatively recent. They were hot topics of public discourse, academic and legal theorizing, and political agitation from the Industrial Revolution through the New Deal. Now they are the province of members of marginalized academic subfields—labor historians, labor law scholars, and some labor economists—along with a few labor lawyers and labor activists.

Our currently dominant tools for discerning our work lives were manufactured before the Industrial Revolution and originally designed as viewfinders to the future. They were rejected as useless by organized labor movements that arose in recognition of the fundamental irreversible changes in workers' prospects brought about by the Industrial Revolution. They have been redeployed since the grave decline of organized labor movements, but now as blinders on our actual institutional landscape of work. We need different instruments to discern the normatively relevant features of our current institutions of workplace governance. In particular, we need to revive the concept of *private government*.

Private Government: The Very Idea

Most modern workplaces are private governments. By this, I do not mean merely that they are in the so-called private sector, and have some internal structure of authority—as specified, for instance, in the rules for corporate governance. I refer rather to a particular sort of constitution of government, under which its subjects are unfree.

The notion of *private government* may seem a contradiction in terms. In the impoverished vocabulary of contemporary public discourse, and to a considerable extent in contemporary political philosophy, *government* is often treated as synonymous with the state, which, by supposed definition, is part of the *public sphere*. The supposed counterpart *private sphere* is the place where, it is imagined, government ends, and hence where individual liberty begins. Here is a characteristic expression of this view in U.S. public discourse: "Giving up our very freedom for a system that allow[s] the government to further meddle in our private lives . . . [is] not the answer. . . . Every single thing government does to increase its own power increases the size of *its slice* of the liberty pie. . . . Since there are only two slices, every time the government's slice of the liberty pie grows, the citizens' slice is *reduced*."[4] That is according to Ken Cuccinelli, the former attorney general of Virginia. But nothing hangs on him. He is merely expressing a view widely accepted in public discourse, certainly among libertarians, but not only among them. Let's unpack the confusions.

First, government exists wherever some have the authority to issue orders to others, backed by sanctions, in one or more domains of life.[5] The modern *state* is merely one form of government among others, defined by Max Weber as "a compulsory organization" that asserts a monopoly on determining the legitimate use of force over a territory.[6] Popular usage before the nineteenth century is much clearer about the government/state distinction than we are today. Here is John Adams, replying to Abigail's famous letter asking him to "remember the ladies":

> We have been told that our struggle has loosened the bonds of government every where; that children and apprentices were disobedient; that schools and colleges were grown turbulent; that Indians slighted their guardians, and negroes grew insolent to their masters. But your letter was the first intimation that another tribe, more numerous and powerful than all the rest, were grown discontented. . . . Depend upon it, we know better than to repeal our masculine systems.[7]

Here Adams frankly acknowledges that government is "every where"—parents (and *govern*esses) exercise government over children, masters over apprentices, teachers over students, guardians over Indians, masters over slaves, husbands over wives. We have seen from my previous lecture that this understanding of the scope of government was equally familiar to actors in seventeenth-century England. Now consider the public/private distinction. If something is legitimately kept private *from* you, that means it is none of your business. This entails at least one of the following: you are not entitled to know about it, your interests have no standing in decisions regarding it, you aren't entitled to make decisions regarding it or to hold those who do accountable for the effect their decisions have on you. If it is private *to* you, that means it *is* your business, *and* you may exclude others from making it any of theirs. This entails at least one of the following: you are entitled to keep others from knowing about it; you need not consider others' interests in making decisions regarding it; you are not accountable to others for your decisions regarding it; you are entitled to exclude others from making decisions regarding it.

If something is *public*, that means it is the business of a more or less well-defined group of people (members of *the public*), such that no one is entitled to exclude any member of the group from making it their business. Publicity in the informational sense typically extends much further than publicity with respect to standing, decision making, and accountability. The latter three categories refer to the governance of the thing in question. Its public status, with respect to governance, involves means by which the public asserts standing to make claims regarding its governance, and organizes itself to make collective decisions regarding it, and/or hold accountable the individuals elected or appointed to make such decisions.

Privacy is relative to persons. A thing that is private with respect to some persons may be public with respect to others. A private club is private from nonmembers, but generally a public thing to its members: the club will typically have meetings to which its members are invited, in which they learn about the club's activities and finances, insist that their interests be taken into account in its operations, make decisions about it, and hold officers of the club accountable. It follows that there is no single public sphere or a single private sphere in society. There are many spheres, and which are public or private depends on who you are.[8]

Today we associate the state with "the" public sphere, and things that are not the state's business, but individuals' own business, with "the" private sphere. Insofar as these associations are thought to be inherent, the idea of *private government* would appear to be contradictory. Isn't everything in the *private sphere* part of individual liberty, and everything subject to *public* (government, confusedly limited to state) control a constraint on individual liberty? That is Cuccinelli's idea, which reflects associations entrenched in contemporary public discourse.

But of course the association of the state with the public sphere is not inherent. It is a contingent social achievement of immense importance. The centuries-long struggles for popular sovereignty and a republican form of government are attempts to make the state a public thing: something that is the people's business, transparent to them, servant to their interests, in which they have a voice and the power to hold rulers accountable. Authoritarian governments insist on the opposite—that the affairs of state are the private business of the rulers.

This point generalizes to *all* governments, not just governments run by the state. You are subject to *private government* wherever (1) you are subordinate to authorities who can order you around and sanction you for not complying over some domain of your life, and (2) the authorities treat it as none of your business, across a wide range of cases, what orders it issues or why it sanctions you. A government is private with respect to a subject if it can issue orders, backed by sanctions, to that subject in some domain of that subject's life, and that subject has no say in how that government operates and no standing to demand that their interests be taken into account, other than perhaps in narrowly defined circumstances, in the decisions that government makes. Private government is government that has arbitrary, unaccountable power over those it governs. This of course is a matter of degree. Its powers may be checked in certain ways by other governments, by social norms, and by other pressures.

Note that *the privacy of a government is defined relative to the governed, not relative to the state.* The notion of governments that are kept private from the state is much more familiar: we speak of corporate governance, church governance, and so forth, in referring to legal entities that are private in relation to the state. That notion of private government abstracts from the people who are governed and their relation to these governments. It focuses only on the fact that the state is kept out of decision-making in these governments. My definition of private government focuses on the fact that, in many of these governments, the governed are kept out of decision-making as well.

Now consider the connections of government to freedom. Cuccinelli depicts a zero-sum trade-off between the liberties of the state and those of its citizens. But there are at least three concepts of freedom: negative, positive, and republican. If you have negative freedom, no one is interfering with your actions. If you have positive freedom, you have a rich menu of options effectively accessible to you, given your resources.[9] If you have republican freedom, no one is dominating you—you are subject to no one's arbitrary, unaccountable will.[10] These three kinds of freedom are distinct. A lone person on a desert island has perfect negative and republican freedom, but virtually no positive freedom, because there is nothing to do but eat coconuts. An absolute monarch's favorites may enjoy great negative and positive freedom if he has granted them generous privileges and well-paid sinecures. But they still lack republican freedom, since he can take their perks away and toss them into a dungeon on a whim. Citizens of prosperous social democracies have considerable positive and republican freedom, but are subject to numerous negative liberty constraints, in the form of complex state regulations that constrain their choices in numerous aspects of their lives.

All three kinds of freedom are valuable. There are sound reasons to make trade-offs among them. If we focus purely on negative liberty, and purely concerning rival goods, it *might* seem that Cuccinelli is correct that the size of the liberty pie is fixed: one agent's liberty over rival good *G* would seem to preclude another's liberty over it. But this is to confuse negative *liberties* with *exclusive rights*. There is nothing incoherent about a Hobbesian state of nature, in which everyone has the negative liberty to take, or compete for possession of, every rival good. That would be a social state of perfect negative liberty: it is a state of anarchist communism, in which the world is an unregulated commons. Such a condition would also be catastrophic. Production would collapse if anyone were free to take whatever anyone else had worked to produce. Even the natural resources of the earth would rapidly be depleted in an unregulated commons. Without property rights—rights to exclude others—people would therefore be very poor and insecure. Opportunities—*positive* liberties—are vastly greater with the establishment of a system of property rights.

This is a standard argument for a regime of private property rights. It is impeccable. Yet its logical entailments are often overlooked. Every establishment of a private property *right* entails a correlative duty, coercively enforceable by individuals or the state, that others refrain from meddling with another's property without the owner's permission. Private property rights thus entail massive net losses in negative liberty, relative to the state of maximum negative liberty. If Lalitha has private property in a parcel of land, her liberty over that parcel is secured by an *exclusive right* at the cost of the identical negative liberty of seven billion others over that parcel. If we are good libertarians and insist that the justification of any constraint on liberty must appeal to some other more important liberty, then the libertarian case for private property depends on accepting that positive liberty very often rightly overrides negative liberty. It follows that even massive state constraints on negative liberty (in the form of enforcements of private property rights) can increase total liberty (in an accounting that weights positive liberty more highly than negative, as any accounting that can justify private property in terms of freedom must).

State-enforced constraints on negative liberty can also increase total liberty through their enhancement of republican freedom. This is a venerable argument from the republican tradition: without robust protection of private property rights (which, as we have seen, entail massive net losses of negative liberty), a republican form of government is insecure, because the state is liable to degenerate into despotism, exercising arbitrary power over its subjects. This argument has been carried over in modern libertarian writing.[11]

This form of argument is equally applicable to substate private governments. If one finds oneself subject to private government—a state of republican unfreedom—one can enhance one's freedom by placing negative liberty constraints on the power of one's private governors to order one around or impose sanctions on one's refusal to comply. This may involve state regulation of private governments. For example, a state's imposition of a requirement on employers that they refrain from discriminating against employees on the basis of their sexual orientation or identity enhances the republican and negative freedom of workers to express their sexual identities and choose their sexual and life partners. It also enhances their positive liberties, by enabling more people to move out of the closet, and thereby increasing opportunities for LGBT people to engage with others of like sexual orientation. The state's imposition of negative liberty constraints on some people can thereby enhance all three liberties of many more.

Private government is, thus, a perfectly coherent concept. To grasp it, we need to reject the false narrowing of the scope of government to the state, recognize that one's liberty can be constrained by private governors in domains of activity kept private from the state, and that increased state constraints on people's negative liberties can generate massive net gains in individual positive and republican freedoms. It can even generate net gains in their negative liberties, to the extent that the people being constrained by the state are private governors over others.

Workplace Government and the Theory of the Firm as Ideological Blinder

Employees are pervasively subject to private government, as I have defined it. Why is this so? As far as the legal authority of the employer to govern employees was concerned, the Industrial Revolution did not mark a significant break. Legally speaking, employers have always been authoritarian rulers, as an extension of their patriarchal rights to govern their households.

The Industrial Revolution moved the primary site of paid work from the household to the factory. In principle, this could have been a liberating moment, insofar as it opened the possibility of separating the governance of the workplace from the governance of the home. Yet industrial employers retained their legal entitlement to govern their employees' domestic lives. In the early twentieth century, the Ford Motor Company established a Sociological Department, dedicated to inspecting employees' homes unannounced, to ensure that they were leading orderly lives. Workers were eligible for Ford's famous $5 daily wage only if they kept their homes clean, ate diets deemed healthy, abstained from drinking, used the bathtub appropriately, did not take in boarders, avoided spending too much on foreign relatives, and were assimilated to American cultural norms.[12]

Workers today might breathe a sigh of relief, except that most are still subject to employer governance of their private lives. In some cases, this is explicit, as in employer-provided health insurance plans. Under the Affordable Care Act (ACA), employers may impose a 30 percent premium penalty on covered workers if they do not comply with employer-imposed wellness programs, which may prescribe exercise programs, diets, and abstinence from alcohol and other substances. In accordance with this provision, Penn State University recently threatened to impose a $100 per month surcharge on workers who did not answer a health survey that included questions about their marital situation, sexual conduct, pregnancy plans, and personal finances.[13] In other cases, employer authority over workers' off-duty lives is implicit, a by-product of the employment-at-will rule: since employers may fire workers for any or no reason, they may fire them for their sexual activities, partner choice, or any other choice workers think of as private from their employer, unless the state has enacted a law specifically forbidding employer discrimination on these grounds. Workplace authoritarianism is still with us.

The pro-market egalitarian aspiration toward nearly universal self-employment aimed to liberate workers from such governance by opening opportunities for nearly everyone to become their own boss. Why did it fail? Why are workers subject to dictatorship? Within economics, the theory of the firm is supposed to answer this question. It purports to offer politically neutral, technical, economic reasons why most production is undertaken by hierarchical organizations, with workers subordinate to bosses, rather than by autonomous individual workers. The theory of the firm contains important insights into the organization of production in advanced economies. However, it fails to explain the sweeping scope of authority that employers have over workers. What is worse, its practitioners sometimes even *deny* that workers lie under the authority of their bosses, in terms that reflect and reinforce an illusion of workers' freedom that also characterizes much of public discourse. Both the theory of the firm, and public discourse, are missing an important reality: that workers are subject to their employers' *private government.*

The pro-market egalitarian dream failed in part due to economies of scale. The technological changes that drove the Industrial Revolution involved huge concentrations of capital. A steam-powered cotton mill, steel foundry, cement or chemical factory, or railway must be worked by many hands. The case is no different for modern workplaces such as airports, hospitals, pharmaceutical labs, and computer assembly factories, as well as lower-tech workplaces such as amusement parks, slaughterhouses, conference hotels, and big-box retail stores. The greater efficiency of production using large, indivisible capital inputs explains why few individual workers can afford to supply their own capital. It explains why, contrary to the pro-market egalitarian hope, the enterprises responsible for most production are not sole proprietorships.

But economies of scale do not explain why production is not managed by independent contractors acting without external supervision, who rent their capital. One could imagine a manufacturing enterprise renting its floor space and machinery and supplying materials to a set of self-employed independent contractors. Each contractor would produce a part or stage of the product for sale to contractors at the next stage of production. The final contractor would sell the finished product to wholesalers, or perhaps back to the capital supplier. Some New England factories operated on a system like this from the Civil War to World War I. They were superseded by hierarchically organized firms. According to the theory of the firm, this is due to the excessive costs of contracting between suppliers of factors of production.[14] In the failed New England system, independent contractors faced each other in a series of bilateral monopolies, which led to opportunistic negotiations. The demand to periodically renegotiate rates led contractors to hoard information and delay innovation for strategic reasons. Independent contractors wore out the machinery too quickly, failed to tightly coordinate their production with workers at other stages of production (leading to excess inventory of intermediate products), and lacked incentives to innovate, both with respect to saving materials and with respect to new products.[15]

The modern firm solves these problems by replacing contractual relations among workers, and between workers and owners of other factors of production, with centralized authority. A manager, or hierarchy of managers, issues orders to workers in pursuit of centralized objectives. This enables close coordination of different workers and internalizes the benefits of all types of innovation within the firm as a whole. Managers can monitor workers to ensure that they work hard, cooperate with fellow workers, and do not waste capital. Because they exercise open-ended authority over workers, they can redeploy workers' efforts as needed to implement innovations, replace absentees, and deal with unforeseen difficulties. Authority relations eliminate the costs associated with constant negotiation and contracting among the participants in the firm's production. To put the point another way, the key to the superior efficiency of hierarchy is the open-ended authority of managers. It is impossible to specify in advance all of the contingencies that may require an alteration in an initial understanding of what a worker must do. Efficient employment contracts are therefore necessarily incomplete: they do not specify precisely everything a worker might be asked to do.

While this theory explains why firms exist and why they are constituted by hierarchies of authority, it does not explain the sweeping scope of employers' authority over workers in the United States. It does not explain, for example, why employers continue to have authority over workers' off-duty lives, given that their choice of sexual partner, political candidate, or Facebook posting has nothing to do with productive efficiency. Even worse, theorists of the firm appear not to even recognize how authoritarian firm governance is. Major theorists soft-pedal or even deny the very authority they are supposed to be trying to explain.

Consider Ronald Coase, the originator of the theory of the firm. He acknowledges that firms are "islands of conscious power."[16] The employment contract is one in which the worker "agrees to obey the directions of an entrepreneur." But, he insists, "the essence of the contract is that it should only state the limits to the powers of the entrepreneur."[17] This suggests that the limits of the employer's powers are an object of negotiation or at least communication between the parties. In the vast majority of cases, outside the contexts of collective bargaining or for higher-level employees, this is not true. Most workers are hired without any negotiation over the content of the employer's authority, and without a written or oral contract specifying any limits to it. If they receive an employee handbook indicating such limits, the inclusion of a simple disclaimer (which is standard practice) is sufficient to nullify any implied contract exception to at-will employment in most states.[18] No wonder they are shocked and outraged when their boss fires them for being too attractive,[19] for failing to show up at a political rally in support of the boss's favored political candidate,[20] even because their daughter was raped by a friend of the boss.[21]

What, then, determines the scope and limits of the employer's authority, if it is not a meeting of minds of the parties? The state does so, through a complex system of laws—not only labor law, but laws regulating corporate governance, workplace safety, fringe benefits, discrimination, and other matters. In the United States, the default employment contract is employment at will. There are a few exceptions in federal law to this doctrine, notably concerning discrimination, family and medical leave, and labor union activity. For the most part, however, at-will employment, which entitles employers to fire workers for any or no reason, grants the employer sweeping legal authority not only over workers' lives at work but also over their off-duty conduct. Under the employment-at-will baseline, workers, in effect, cede *all* of their rights to their employers, except those specifically guaranteed to them by law, for the duration of the employment relationship. Employers' authority over workers, outside of collective bargaining and a few other contexts, such as university professors' tenure, is sweeping, arbitrary, and unaccountable—not subject to notice, process, or appeal. The *state* has established the constitution of the government of the workplace: it is a form of private government.

Resistance to recognizing this reality appears to be widespread among theorists of the firm. Here, for example, is what Armen Alchian and Harold Demsetz say in their classic paper on the subject:

> It is common to see the firm characterized by the power to settle issues by fiat, by authority, or by disciplinary action. . . . This is delusion. The firm . . . has no power of fiat, no authority, no disciplinary action any different in the slightest degree from ordinary market contracting between any two people. I can "punish" you only by withdrawing future business or by seeking redress in the courts for any failure to honor our exchange agreement. That is exactly all that any employer can do. He can fire or sue, just as I can fire my grocer by stopping purchases from him or sue him for delivering faulty products. What then is the content of the presumed power to manage and assign workers to various tasks? Exactly the same as one little consumer's power to manage and assign his grocer to various tasks. . . . To speak of managing, directing, or assigning workers to various tasks is a deceptive way of noting that the employer continually is involved in renegotiation of contracts on terms that must be acceptable to both parties. Telling an employee to type this letter rather than to file that document is like telling a grocer to sell me this brand of tuna rather than that brand of bread. I have no contract to continue to purchase

from the grocer and neither the employer nor the employee is bound by any contractual obligations to continue their relationship.[22]

Alchian and Demsetz appear to be claiming that wherever individuals are free to exit a relationship, authority cannot exist within it. This is like saying that Mussolini was not a dictator, because Italians could emigrate. While emigration rights may give governors an interest in voluntarily restraining their power, such rights hardly dissolve it.[23]

Alternatively, their claim might be that where the only sanctions for disobedience are exile, or a civil suit, authority does not exist. That would come as a surprise to those subject to the innumerable state regulations that are backed only by civil sanctions. Nor would a state regulation lack authority if the only sanction for violating it were to force one out of one's job. Finally, managers have numerous other sanctions at their disposal besides firing and suing: they can and often do demote employees; cut their pay; assign them inconvenient hours or too many or too few hours; assign them more dangerous, dirty, menial, or grueling tasks; increase their pace of work; set them up to fail; and, within very broad limits, humiliate and harass them.

Perhaps the thought is that where consent mediates the relationship between the parties, the relationship cannot be one of subordination to authority. That would be a surprise to the entire social contract tradition, which is precisely about how the people can consent to government. Or is the idea that authority exists only where subordinates obey orders blindly and automatically? But then it exists hardly anywhere. Even the most repressive regimes mostly rely on means besides sheer terror and brainwashing to elicit compliance with their orders, focusing more on persuasion and rewards.

Alchian and Demsetz may be hoodwinked by the superficial symmetry of the employment contract: under employment-at-will, workers, too, may quit for any or no reason. This leads them to represent quitting as equivalent to firing one's boss. But workers have no power to remove the boss from his position within the firm. And quitting often imposes even greater costs on workers than being fired does, for it makes them ineligible for unemployment insurance. It is an odd kind of countervailing power that workers supposedly have to check their bosses' power, when they typically suffer more from imposing it than they would suffer from the worst sanction bosses can impose on them. Threats, to be effective, need to be credible.

The irony is that Alchian and Demsetz are offering a theory of the firm. The question the theory is supposed to answer is why production is not handled entirely by market transactions among independent, self-employed people, but rather by authority relations. That is, it is supposed to explain why the hope of pro-market pre–Industrial Revolution egalitarians did not pan out. Alchian and Demsetz cannot bear the full authoritarian implications of recognizing the boundary between the market and the firm, even in a paper devoted to explaining it. So they attempt to extend the metaphor of the market to the internal relations of the firm and pretend that every interaction at work is mediated by negotiation between managers and workers. Yet the whole point of the firm, according to the theory, is to eliminate the costs of markets—of setting internal prices via negotiation over every transaction among workers and between workers and managers.

Alchian and Demsetz are hardly alone. Michael Jensen and William Meckling agree with them that authority has nothing to do with the firm; it is merely a nexus of contracts among independent individuals.[24] John Tomasi, writing today, continues to promote the image of employees as akin to independent contractors, freely negotiating the terms of their contract with their employers, to obtain work conditions tailor-made to their idiosyncratic specifications.[25] While workers at the top of the corporate hierarchy enjoy such freedom, as well as a handful of elite athletes, entertainers, and star academics, Tomasi ignores the fact that the vast majority of workers not represented by unions do not negotiate terms of the employer's authority at all. Why would employers bother, when, by state fiat, workers automatically cede all liberties not reserved to them by the state, upon accepting an offer of work?

Not just theorists of the firm, but public discourse too, tend to represent employees as if they were independent contractors.[26] This makes it seem as if the workplace is a continuation of arm's-length market transactions, as if the labor contract were no different from a purchase from Smith's butcher, baker, or brewer. Alchian and Demsetz are explicit about this, in drawing the analogy of the employment relation with the customer–grocer relation. But the butcher, baker, and brewer remain independent from their customers after selling their goods. In the employment contract, by contrast, the workers cannot separate themselves from the labor they have sold; in purchasing command over labor, employers purchase command over people.

What accounts for this error? The answer is, in part, that a representation of what egalitarians hoped market society would deliver for workers before the Industrial Revolution has been blindly carried over to the post–Industrial Revolution world. People continue to deploy the same justification of market society—that it would secure the personal independence of workers from arbitrary authority—long after it failed to deliver on its original aspiration. The result is a kind of political hemiagnosia: like those patients who cannot perceive one-half of their bodies, a large class of libertarian-leaning thinkers and politicians, with considerable public following, cannot perceive half of the economy: they cannot perceive the half that takes place *beyond* the market, *after* the employment contract is accepted.

This tendency was reinforced by a narrowing of egalitarian vision in the transition to the Industrial Revolution. While the Levellers and other radicals of the mid-seventeenth century agitated against all kinds of arbitrary government, Thomas Paine mainly narrowed his critique to state abuses. Similarly, the Republican Party kept speaking mainly on behalf of the interests of businesspeople and those who hoped to be in business for themselves, even after it was clear that the overwhelming majority of workers had no realistic prospect of attaining this status, and that the most influential businesspeople were not, as Lincoln hoped, sole proprietors (with at most a few employees, the majority of whom were destined to rise to self-employed status after a few years), but managers in large organizations, governing workers destined to be wage laborers for their entire working lives. Thus, a political agenda that once promised equalizing as well as liberating outcomes turned into one that reinforced private, arbitrary, unaccountable government over the vast majority.

Finally, nineteenth-century laissez-faire liberals, with their bizarre combination of hostility toward state power and enthusiasm for hyperdisciplinary total institutions, attempted to reconcile these contradictory tendencies by limiting their focus to the entry and exit conditions of the labor contract, while blackboxing what actually went on in the factories. In fact, they did drive a dramatic improvement in workers' freedom of entry and exit.[27] Under the traditional common law of master and servant, employees were bound to their employers by contracts of one year (apprentices and indentured servants for longer), could quit before then only on pain of losing all their accrued wages, and were not entitled to keep wages from moonlighting. Other employers were forbidden to bid for their labor while they were still under contract.[28] Workers were liberated from these constraints over the course of the nineteenth century.[29]

This liberation, as is well-known, was a double-edged sword. Employers, too, were liberated from any obligation to employ workers. As already noted, the worst the workers could do to the boss often involved suffering at least as much as the worst the boss could do to them. For the bulk of workers, who lived at the bottom of the hierarchy, this was not much of a threat advantage, unless it was exercised collectively in a strike. They had no realistic hope under these conditions for liberation from workplace authoritarianism.

No wonder a central struggle of British workers in the mid-nineteenth century was for limits on the length of the working day—even more than for higher wages. This was true, even though workers at this period of the Industrial Revolution were suffering through "Engels's pause"—the first fifty to sixty years of the Industrial Revolution during which wages failed to grow.[30] My focus, like theirs, is not on issues of wages or distributive justice. It is on workers' freedom. If the Industrial Revolution meant they could not be their own bosses at work, at least they could try to limit the length of the working day so that they would have some hours during which they could choose for themselves, rather than follow someone else's orders.[31]

That was an immediate aim of European workers' movements in the mid-nineteenth century. As the century unfolded, workers largely abandoned their pro-market, individualistic egalitarian dream and turned to socialist, collectivist alternatives—that is, to restructuring the internal governance of the workplace. The problem was that the options open to workers consisted almost exclusively of private governments. Laissez-faire liberals, touting the freedom of the free market, told workers: choose your Leviathan. That is like telling the citizens of the Communist bloc of Eastern Europe that their freedom could be secured by a right to emigrate to any country—as long as they stayed behind the Iron Curtain. Population movements would likely have put some pressure on Communist rulers to soften their rule. But why should Leviathan set the baseline against which competition took place? No liberal or libertarian would be satisfied with a competitive equilibrium set against this baseline, where the choice of state governments is concerned. Workers' movements rejected it for nonstate governments as well.

To their objection, libertarians and laissez-faire liberals had no credible answer. Let us not fool ourselves into supposing that the competitive equilibrium of labor relations was ever established by politically neutral market forces mediated by pure freedom of contract, with nothing but the free play of individuals' idiosyncratic preferences determining the outcome. This is a delusion as great as the one that imagines that the workplace is not authoritarian. Every competitive equilibrium is established against a background assignment of property rights and other rights established by the state. The state supplies the indispensable legal infrastructure of developed economies as a kind of public good, and is needed to do so to facilitate cooperation on the vast scales that characterize today's rich and sophisticated economies.[32] Thus, it is the state that establishes the default constitution of workplace governance. It is a form of authoritarian, private government, in which, under employment-at-will, workers cede *all* their rights to their employers, except those specifically reserved for them by law.

Freedom of entry and exit from any employment relation is not sufficient to justify the outcome. To see this, consider an analogous case for the law of coverture, which the state had long established as the default marriage contract.[33] Under coverture, a woman, upon marrying her husband, lost all rights to own property and make contracts in her own name. Her husband had the right to confine her movements, confiscate any wages she might earn, beat her, and rape her. Divorce was very difficult to obtain. The marriage contract was valid only if voluntarily accepted by both parties. It was a contract into subjection, entailing the wife's submission to the private government of her husband. Imagine a modification of this patriarchal governance regime, allowing either spouse to divorce at will and allowing any clause of the default contract to be altered by a prenuptial agreement. This is like the modification that laissez-faire liberals added to the private government of the workplace. Women would certainly have sufficient reason to object that their liberties would still not be respected under this modification, in that it preserves a patriarchal baseline, in which men still hold virtually all the cards. It would allow a lucky few to escape subjection to their husbands, but that is not enough to justify the patriarchal authority the vast majority of men would retain over their wives.[34] Consent to an option within a set cannot justify the option set itself.

Back to the Future

My historical investigation explains why a certain libertarian way of thinking about market society and its promise made considerable sense in its original context prior to the Industrial Revolution, and why it was reasonable for egalitarians to support it at that time. But the Industrial Revolution destroyed the context in which that vision made sense. The new context perverted what was once a liberating, egalitarian vision into support for pervasive workplace authoritarianism—arbitrary, hierarchical, private government. The evolving rhetoric of laissez-faire liberalism that arose in the nineteenth century papered over the real issues and represented, in Orwellian fashion, subjection as freedom.

Workers' movements from the mid-nineteenth century through World War II were not fooled by this.[35] That is not to say that they all had sound ideas for how to solve the problem. I have no space to recount the follies of democratic state socialism.[36] Nor do I have space to recount the catastrophes of state communism, which were dominated by the same totalitarian vision of the original designers of total institutions—only dramatically scaled up, more violent, and unmixed with any skepticism about state power. Like the original designers, state communists looked to ideals of neither liberty nor equality, but rather to utilitarian progress and the perfectibility of human beings under the force of private government.

My point is rather that, with the drastic decline of organized labor, and especially with the triumph of ostensibly free markets since the end of the Cold War, public and academic discourse has largely lost sight of the problem that organized workers in the nineteenth century saw clearly: the pervasiveness of private government at work. Here most of us are, toiling under the authority of communist dictators, and we do not see the reality for what it is.

No doubt many of us, especially most of those who are reading these lectures, do not find the situation so bad. My readers, most likely, are tenured or tenure-track professors, who, almost uniquely among unorganized workers in the United States, enjoy due process rights and a level of autonomy at work that is unmatched almost anywhere else among employees.[37] Or, if they are college students or graduates, they are or likely will be the dictators or higher-ranked officials of private governments. Or they will escape the system and belong to the thin ranks of the self-employed who have no employees of their own. The people I am worried about are the 25 percent of employees who understand that they are subject to dictatorship at work,[38] and the other 55 percent or so who are neither securely self-employed nor upper-level managers, nor the tiny elite tier of nonmanagerial stars (athletes, entertainers, superstar academics) who have the power to dictate employment contracts to their specification, nor even the ever-shrinking class of workers under ever-retrenching collective bargaining agreements. That 55 percent is only one arbitrary and oppressive managerial decision away from realizing what the 25 percent already know. But this 80 percent receives almost no recognition in contemporary public and academic discourse.

I do not claim that private governments at work are as powerful as states. Their sanctioning powers are lower, and the costs of emigration from oppressive private governments are generally lower than the costs of emigration from states. Yet private governments impose a far more minute, exacting, and sweeping regulation of employees than democratic states do in any domain outside of prisons and the military. Private governments impose controls on workers that are unconstitutional for democratic states to impose on citizens who are not convicts or in the military.

The negative liberties most workers enjoy de facto are considerably greater than the ones they are legally entitled to under their employers. Market pressures, social norms, lack of interest, and simple decency keep most employers from exercising the full scope of their authority. We should care nevertheless about the insecurity of employees' liberty. They work in a state of republican unfreedom, their liberties vulnerable to cancellation without justification, notice, process, or appeal. That they enjoy substantially greater negative liberty than they are legally entitled to no more justifies their lack of republican liberty than the fact that most wives enjoyed greater freedoms than they were legally entitled to justified coverture—or even coverture modified by free divorce.

Suppose people find themselves under private government. This is a state of republican unfreedom, of subjection to the arbitrary will of another. It is also usually a state of substantial constraints on negative liberty. By what means could people attain their freedom? One way would be to end subjection to government altogether. When the government is a state, this is the anarchist answer. We have seen that when the government is an employer, the answer of many egalitarians before the Industrial Revolution was to advance a property regime that promotes self-employment, perhaps even to make self-employment a nearly universally accessible opportunity, at least for men. This amounts to promoting anarchy as the primary form of workplace order.

The theory of the firm explains why this approach cannot preserve the productive advantages of large-scale production. Some kind of incompletely specified authority over groups of workers is needed to replace market relations within the firm. However, the theory of the firm, although it explains the necessity of hierarchy, neither explains nor justifies private government in the workplace. That the constitution of workplace government is both arbitrary and dictatorial is not dictated by efficiency or freedom of contract, but rather by the state. Freedom of contract no more explains the equilibrium workplace constitution than freedom to marry explained women's subjection to patriarchy under coverture.

In other words, in the great contest between individualism and collectivism regarding the mode of production, collectivism won, decisively. Now nearly all production is undertaken by teams of workers using large, indivisible forms of capital equipment held in common. The activities of these teams are governed by managers according to a centralized production plan. This was an outcome of the Industrial Revolution, and equally much embraced by capitalists and socialists. That advocates of capitalism continue to speak as if their preferred system of production upholds "individualism" is simply a symptom of institutional hemiagnosia, the misdeployment of a hopeful preindustrial vision of what market society would deliver as if it described our current reality, which replaces market relations with governance relations across wide domains of production.

Workers in the nineteenth century turned from individualistic to collectivist solutions to workplace governance because they saw that interpersonal authority—governments over groups of workers—was inescapable in the new industrial order. If government is inescapable or necessary for solving certain important problems, the only way to make people free under that government is to make that government a public thing, accountable to the governed. The task is to replace private government with public government.

When the government is a state, we have some fairly good ideas of how to proceed: the entire history of democracy under the rule of law is a series of experiments in how to make the government of the state a public thing, and the people free under the state. These experiments continue to this day.

But what if the government is an employer? Here matters are more uncertain. There are four general strategies for advancing and protecting the liberties and interests of the governed under any type of government: (1) exit, (2) the rule of law, (3) substantive constitutional rights, and (4) voice. Let us consider each in turn.

Exit is usually touted as a prime libertarian strategy for protecting individual rights. By forcing governments to compete for subjects, exit rights put pressure on governments to offer their subjects better deals. "The defense against oppressive hours, pay, working conditions, or treatment is the right to change employers."[39] Given this fact, it is surprising how comfortable some libertarians are with the validity of contracts into slavery, from which exit is disallowed.[40] In their view, freedom of contract trumps the freedom of individuals under government, or even the freedom to leave that government. While contracts into slavery and peonage are no longer valid, other contractual barriers to exit are common and growing. Noncompete clauses, which bar employees from working for other employers in the same industry for a period of years, have spread from technical professions (where nearly half of employees are subject to them) to jobs such as sandwich maker, pesticide sprayer, summer camp counselor, and hairstylist.[41] While employers can no longer hold workers in bondage, they can imprison workers' human capital. California is one of the few states that prohibit noncompete clauses. As the dynamism of its economy proves, such contractual barriers to exit are not needed for economic growth, and probably undermine it.[42] There should be a strong legal presumption against such barriers to exit, to protect workers' freedom to exit their employers' government.

The rule of law is a complex ideal encompassing several protections of subjects' liberties: (a) Authority may be exercised only through laws duly passed and publicized in advance, rather than arbitrary orders issued without any process. (b) Subjects are at liberty to do anything not specifically prohibited by law. (c) Laws are generally applicable to everyone in similar circumstances. (d) Subjects have rights of due process before suffering any sanctions for noncompliance. Not all of these protections, which were devised with state authority in mind, can be readily transferred to the employment context. Most of the solutions to problems the state must address involve regulations that leave open to individuals a vast array of options for selecting both ends and means. By contrast, efficient production nearly always requires close coordination of activities according to centralized objectives, directed by managers exercising discretionary authority. This frequently entails that the authority of managers over workers be both intensive (limiting workers to highly particular movements and words, not allowing them to pursue their own personal objectives at work or even to select their own means to a prescribed end) and incompletely specified. The state imposes traffic laws that leave people free to choose their own destinations, routes, and purposes. Walmart tells its drivers what they have to pick up, when and where they have to deliver it, and what route they have to take. In addition, managers need incompletely specified authority to rapidly reassign different tasks to different workers to address new circumstances. Finally, excessively costly procedural protections against firing also discourage hiring. All these obstacles to applying rule-of-law protections in the workplace empower employers to abuse their authority, subject workers to humiliating treatment, and impose excessive constraints on their freedom.

At the same time, it is easy to exaggerate the obstacles to imposing rule-of-law protections at work. Larger organizations generally have employee handbooks and standard practice guides that streamline authority along legalistic lines. Equal protection and due process rights already exist for workers in larger organizations with respect to limited issues. A worker who has been sexually harassed by her boss normally has recourse to intrafirm procedures for resolving her complaint. Such protections reflect a worldwide "blurring of boundaries" among business, nonprofit, and state organizations, which appears to be driven not simply by legal changes, but by cultural imperatives of scientific management and ideas of individual rights and organizational responsibilities.[43] Some but not all of these managerial developments are salutary. They are proper subjects of investigation for political theory, once we get beyond the subject's narrow focus on the state.

A just workplace constitution should incorporate basic constitutional rights, akin to a bill of rights against employers. To some extent, the Fair Labor Standards Act, anti-discrimination laws, and other workplace regulations already serve this function. A workers' bill of rights could be strengthened by the addition of more robust protections of workers' freedom to engage in off-duty activities, such as exercising their political rights, free speech,[44] and sexual choices. Similar protections for employee privacy could be extended in the workplace during work breaks. The Occupational Safety and Health Administration (OSHA) prohibitions of particularly degrading, dangerous, and onerous working conditions can be viewed as part of a workers' bill of rights. Nabisco once threatened its female production line workers with three-day suspensions for using the bathroom, and ordered them to urinate in their clothes instead.[45] It was only in 1998 that OSHA issued a regulation requiring employers to recognize workers' right to use a bathroom, after cases such as Nabisco's aroused public outrage. Workers in Europe are protected from harassment of all kinds by anti-mobbing laws.[46] This gives them far more robust workplace constitutional rights than workers in the United States, who may be legally harassed as long as their harassers do not discriminate by race, gender, or other protected identities in choosing their victims.

There are limits, however, to how far a bill of rights can go in protecting workers from abuse. Because they prescribe uniformity across workplaces, they can at best offer a minimal floor. In practice, they are also grossly underenforced for the least advantaged workers.[47] Furthermore, such laws do not provide for worker participation in governance at the firm level. They merely impose limits on employer dictatorship.

For these reasons, there is no adequate substitute for recognizing workers' voice in their government. Voice can more readily adapt workplace rules to local conditions than state regulations can, while incorporating respect for workers' freedom, interests, and dignity. Just because workplace governance requires a hierarchy of offices does not mean that higher officeholders must be unaccountable to the governed, or that the governed should not play any role in managerial decision-making. In the United States, two models for workers' voice have received the most attention: workplace democracy and labor unions. Workplace democracy, in the form of worker-owned and -managed firms, has long stood as an ideal for many egalitarians.[48] While much could be done to devise laws more accommodating of this structure, some of its costs may be difficult to surmount. In particular, the costs of negotiation among workers with asymmetrical interests (for example, due to possession of different skills) appear to be high.[49]

In the United States, collective bargaining has been the primary way workers have secured voice within the government of the workplace. However, even at its peak in 1954, only 28.3 percent of workers were represented by a labor union.[50] Today, only 11.1 percent of all workers and 6.6 percent of private sector workers are represented.[51] Although laws could be revised to make it easier for workers to organize into a union, this does not address difficulties inherent to the U.S. labor union model. The U.S. model organizes workers at the firm level rather than the industry level. Firms vigorously resist unionization to avoid a competitive disadvantage with nonunionized firms.[52] Labor unions also impose inefficiencies due to their monopoly power.[53] They also take an adversarial stance toward management—one that makes not only managers but also many workers uncomfortable. At the same time, they often provide the only effective voice employees have in workplace governance.

It is possible to design a workplace constitution in which workers have a nonadversarial voice in workplace governance, without raising concerns about monopolization. The overwhelming majority of workers in the United States would like to have such a voice: 85 percent would like firm governance to be "run jointly" by management and workers.[54] In the United States, such a constitution is illegal under the National Labor Relations Act, which prohibits company unions. Yet this structure is commonplace in Europe. Germany's system of codetermination, begun in the Weimar era and elaborately developed since World War II, offers one highly successful model.[55]

It is not my intention in this lecture to defend any particular model of worker participation in firm governance. My point is rather to expose a deep failure in current ways of thinking about how government fits into Americans' lives. We do not live in the market society imagined by Paine and Lincoln, which offered an appealing vision of what a free society of equals would look like, combining individualistic libertarian and egalitarian ideals. Government is everywhere, not just in the form of the state, but even more pervasively in the workplace. Yet public discourse and much of political theory pretends that this is not so. It pretends that the constitution of workplace government is somehow the object of voluntary negotiation between workers and employers. This is true only for a tiny proportion of privileged workers. The vast majority are subject to private, authoritarian government, not through their own choice, but through laws that have handed nearly all authority to their employers.

It is high time that public discourse acknowledged this reality and the costs to workers' freedom and dignity that private government imposes on them. It is high time that political theorists turned their attention to the private governments of the workplace. Since the Levellers, egalitarian social movements have insisted that if government is necessary, it must be made a public thing to all the governed—accountable to them, responsive to their interests, and open to their participation. They were shrewd enough to recognize the pervasiveness of private government in their lives. It is time to go back to the future in recovering such recognition and experimenting with ways to remedy it.

Comments

Chapter 3

Learning from the Levellers?

Ann Hughes

As the most recent historian of the Levellers has declared, "the Levellers can seem uncannily modern."[1] In late October 1647, Colonel Thomas Rainborough, one of the Leveller sympathizers at the Putney debates, insisted in an argument about the extent of the franchise in a reimagined and reconstructed English polity: "really I think that the poorest he that is in England hath a life to live as the greatest he; and therefore truly, sir, I think it's clear that every man that is to live under a government ought first by his own consent to put himself under that government; and I do think that the poorest man in England is not at all bound in a strict sense to that government that he has not had a voice to put himself under."[2] The Putney debates, held in a London suburban church, involved the commanders and soldiers of the English Parliament's victorious army, and some civilian associates, in discussions of the possible settlement of the kingdom following the decisive defeat of Charles I in a traumatic and bloody civil war; they demonstrate, among other things, the capacity of relatively ordinary men for intellectual vision and political resourcefulness. Professor Anderson notes the "intellectual depth and seriousness" of these debates (Lecture 1, note 9); their words still resonate for contemporary egalitarians.

That this call for a broad manhood suffrage—the poorest "he" (and we should pause a little over the "he")—was couched in economic terms is something to which I will return. Professor Anderson offers an eloquent, perceptive, moving, and challenging account of the seventeenth-century English Levellers as egalitarian thinkers and as activists. They offer us resources for thinking about our continuing dilemmas of how to argue and work for a fairer society. Her first lecture is an exemplary demonstration of the deployment of historical material as a storehouse of the imagination, and a legacy for the present. Professor Anderson suggests that an apparently paradoxical Leveller commitment to free exchange through the market could nonetheless suggest how we might conceive of equality as more than a material issue, as a matter of esteem, standing, and authority, in Anderson's terms. Furthermore, the Levellers, as a pioneering "egalitarian social movement," are the foundation for Anderson's project of recovering a normative egalitarianism for the contemporary world.

Leveller petitions, campaigns, and manifestos did indeed include attacks on the great monopoly trading companies. Their "great" petition of September 1648 demanded of the English Parliament, as its tenth clause, "that you would have freed all trade and merchandising from all monopolizing and engrossing by Companies and others."[3] Their pamphlets often endorsed a variety of political and social campaigns, including support for provincial merchants trying to break in to London-dominated trades.[4] Like more recent free-marketeers, Levellers were anxious to constrain the power of the "state," even that new state they sought to bring into being. As Rainborough was speaking at Putney, army radicals issued the first version of the "Agreement of the People," a manifesto for the remaking of the English polity that has come to define our understanding of the Leveller movement. The current Parliament, which had failed to deliver on its promises to the people, was to be replaced through a direct process of participation and consent. The Agreement was founded on trust in the capacity of ordinary (male) political actors, and a profound suspicion of concentration of power in all its forms: it called for the dissolution of the present Parliament, "to prevent the many inconveniences apparently arising from the long continuance of the same persons in authority"; then "the people" would "of course" choose a Parliament every two years. Constituencies were to be established proportionately to their population, which implied universal manhood suffrage. This new Representative was charged with the passing and enforcing of law, the making of war and peace, and the appointing of office holders. The framers of the Agreement thus proposed wide authority for this body but hastened immediately to limit its scope. Following elections, "the power of this and all future Representatives of this nation is inferior only to theirs who choose them"; except for "whatsoever is not expressly or impliedly reserved by the represented to themselves." Certain powers could not be resigned by the people to their Representative, and these "whatsoevers" were extremely significant. The first "reservation," probably the most important, concerned religious liberty: the Representative was to have no power over "matters of religion . . . because therein we cannot remit or exceed a tittle of what our consciences dictate to be the mind of God, without wilful sin." In modern political analysis, control over military affairs is usually central to conceptions of the state, but even here the Levellers sought to curtail the Representative's powers: the second "reservation" declared that conscription for military service was "against our freedom," although the Agreement acknowledged that "money (the sinews of war) being always at their disposal," the Representative was unlikely to "want numbers of men apt enough to engage in any just cause."[5] The Levellers' profound suspicion of state power is revealed in the May 1649 final version of the Agreement of the People, which called for annual Parliaments, with no permanent executive allowed; the state would in effect be run by temporary committees of each Parliament.[6]

The Levellers' resistance to tyranny, their commitment to freedom, popular consent, and the individual conscience, and their consistent opposition to the monopolization of power, whether in the state, the law, the economy, or the church, offer, as Professor Anderson's first lecture demonstrated, an inspiring and still relevant egalitarian vision for those on the left. These Tanner lectures were presented shortly after "lovers of liberty and justice in Britain" used Rainborough's words at Putney to inspire their opposition to a Global Law Summit denounced as "a shameless festival of corporate networking."[7] As the lectures were given, British activists, film-makers, songwriters, and historians were celebrating the four-hundredth anniversary of the birth of John Lilburne, the most celebrated Leveller leader. Among these activists were Tariq Ali and Jeremy Corbyn, now the leader of the British Labour Party. John Lilburne is said to be the historical figure Corbyn most admires, while Tariq Ali, like Professor Anderson, has seen the agitation of the 1640s as a resource for thinking about present dilemmas, but he was prompted, not to a defense of market relations but to call for a new "Grand Remonstrance" that would demand the "nationalization" of the railways and public utilities (what British socialists used to call the commanding heights of the economy), returning them to public/state ownership.[8]

Mid-seventeenth-century English history can provide profoundly divergent legacies for our contemporary world. This raises for me, writing as a historian, some difficult issues of how we deploy historical material within other disciplines, and within broader contemporary public discourse. Most historians today want their scholarship to engage with public concerns and even to have an impact on public policy, although they disagree (often bitterly) about how best this can be done.[9] On the other hand, most historians are instinctive or congenital pedants, habitually prone to nit-picking about their specialist areas and periods. Even in these post-postmodern days, after the linguistic turn, when we understand that all accounts of the past are contested and provisional, we are still committed to constructing the most "accurate" or at least plausible version possible, one that most coheres with the surviving evidence. So I do want to say that the Levellers and their seventeenth-century social context were not quite as portrayed in Professor Anderson's first lecture. I do not want to hurl boring, isolated supposed "facts" into our discussions, but I do want to encourage us to think about what difference it makes to our arguments if the historical picture is made a bit more complicated, or even contradictory. Historical material offers raw material for inspiration, and for thought experiments in which we seek alternative directions or means of achieving change. How, though, does this differ from the use of imaginative literature or abstract philosophical concepts? How much does it matter that something—that we, as historians, try to understand as well as we possibly can—really happened, and involved real people? This is an unsophisticated formulation, but I do want to insist on the limits of the real, and on the benefits of acknowledging these limits. Historians' skepticism in the face of the partial, intractable evidence that survives from the past usually produces complex accounts of historical processes; it may be that complexity, rather than straightforward solutions, best serves our current dilemmas.

Within this framework, then, writing as a historian of mid-seventeenth-century England, I want to address three aspects of Professor Anderson's first lecture, suggesting we need a more nuanced or more complicated picture. I will focus especially on the nature of early modern economic and social change in England. How should we characterize it as a society in transition, and how might our characterization affect the potential for the market to be "left"? Second, and more specifically, I want to complicate the notion of the market itself, in its early modern form, and nuance Leveller attitudes to markets and to private property. Finally, because Professor Anderson's lecture raises the question directly, I want to ask where women fit in here, both within the Leveller movement, and when we consider the relationship between "individuals" (put deliberately in quotation marks) in markets.

Professor Anderson, following Adam Smith, structures part of her argument around a positive transition in England, from a feudal society where social relationships were based on fawning servility, to a capitalist market economy, where "masterless men" could potentially achieve autonomy, through reciprocal transactions of exchange conducted on a basis of equal dignity. This is a drastically simplified version of social transformation, but we should probably not judge Smith as a historian; his method is rather the more schematic one of a political economist or even of an avowedly utopian thinker. We need, however, to understand the complexities of how social and economic changes in sixteenth- and seventeenth-century England

affected people like the Levellers, and consequently, the sub-
tleties of how, as a movement, the Levellers responded to these
changes. Within their historical context, the Levellers appear to
be more ambiguous about the potential of this new world. Early
modern England did not experience an Industrial Revolution,
but it did see very significant, dislocating change in the century before the Civil War, and as Anderson shows, the effects
were very diverse. Sections of the population benefited from
rising population and inflation; and from the expansion, spe-
cialization and greater productivity of agriculture, industry, and
commerce. These groups profited from market transactions.
But people with small amounts of land, and insecure tenancies
where profiteering landlords could raise rents or enclose land
for private exploitation, fell by the wayside. They became dependent on wages or languished as "masterless" men; and most
such men were not the self-employed farmers or artisans enjoying independence, as idealistically described in the lecture.
These masterless men were rather vulnerable wage laborers
or vagrants, dependent on individual charity or, increasingly,
on public assistance. The most authoritative social historian of
early modern England, Keith Wrightson, sees production for
the market a risk small households were "constrained to make"
rather than an opportunity.[10] The changes of the sixteenth and
early seventeenth centuries produced poverty on an unprec-
edented scale, and a rising number of households dependent
on wage-labor, during an era of declining real wages. Probably
half the population relied mainly on wage labor by the middle
of the seventeenth century. The national income of England
doubled at least in the century up to 1640, but, as in other periods, the benefits of this expansion were unevenly shared and
the results were greater inequality and increased social polarization. It became less and less likely that an apprenticeship

to an urban trade was a pathway to a comfortable life as an independent artisan or businessman; many hopeful young men faced a lifetime as journeymen or laborers. The Levellers made much of the rights of "freeborn" Englishmen, and their campaigns helped to give the term *free man* some of its modern connotations of individual autonomy and agency, but it also continued to imply someone with specific and exclusive privileges in trade and manufacture as a member of a company or guild. In this sense, barely half of adult males in London were free men by 1640. Economic change and commercialization in practice went in hand-in-hand with increasing state power, to defend English overseas trade, and, most pertinent to our discussions here, to address the problems that resulted from increasing social polarization. As Keith Wrightson has explained, by the mid-seventeenth century, "a commonwealth based upon households had become one in which a substantial segment of the population was no longer able to sustain a household without periodic public assistance, and in which a further substantial minority could not establish an independent household at all."[11] England's unique system of poor relief began as local initiative, subsequently established by national legislation and locally enforced in parishes. The English poor law represented and helped to construct new social hierarchies: by the second half of the seventeenth century, some 40 percent of the population lived in rate-paying households; while 10 percent at least usually were in receipt of relief; with the rest somewhere between the two—too poor to pay the rates, and intermittently dependent on parish help.[12]

It is difficult then to share Adam Smith's benign judgment on social and economic change in early modern England. There were more losers than winners, and most of the Leveller leaders, and many of the cavalry at least in Parliament's army were from the more prosperous sections of this divided society, albeit not from its richest elements; historians use the woolly term the "middling sort."[13] We should not labor this point by connecting men's social programs or political views directly to their social standing, but it is worth noting that Rainborough's advocacy of the political rights of poor men did not reflect his own economic position, for he was the oldest son of a prominent London merchant and naval officer; it was most probably the comradeship of parliamentarian military service that prompted his egalitarian vision. William Walwyn was the Leveller who developed the most extended justification of free trade as "most advantageous to the Commonwealth," but he was himself a freeman of the great Merchant Adventurers' Company and the grandson of a bishop.[14] Levellers were mostly independent householders of the "middling sort"; they could conceive of markets as offering opportunities, but they were also intimately aware of the danger of "declining" into a shameful dependency on charity or wage labor. They would certainly have recognized the force of Adam Smith's comment, quoted in the lecture, that "no one but a beggar chooses to depend chiefly on the benevolence of his fellow citizens." The Levellers sometimes hesitated over adult male suffrage, one spokesman acknowledging at Putney, that: "I conceive the reason why we would exclude apprentices, or servants, or those that take alms, is because they depend upon the will of other men and should be afraid to displease them. For servants and apprentices, *they are included in their masters,* and so for those that receive alms from door to door." In the third and final Agreement of the People, there were political and social exclusions from the franchise: all men of twenty-one and upward "not being servants, or receiving alms, or having served the late king in arms or voluntary contributions" were to vote for the Representative.[15]

The Levellers indeed hated concentrations of power and restrictions on people's freedom, they loathed the ways the rich and powerful could monopolize privilege and manipulate the law, but I wonder how central a free market was to their vision. Their loathing of domination was based on an optimistic view of human nature and of the possibilities of political engagement. In social terms, Leveller proposals owed as much to self-confidence as to experience of oppression, for men of the "middling sort" were accustomed to participation in English legal and political processes (as jurors in counties, or constables and church-wardens in their local communities). Above all, however, Leveller drives for egalitarian social and political forms were the product of exhilarating religious and political struggles. They emerged out of the dramatic, radicalizing experience of fighting and winning a civil war; a war where Parliament had called on the "people" to rally to its cause; where the House of Commons had claimed to be the representative of the people; and where the war had been presented as a struggle for God's true religion, but there was no settled agreement on what true religion actually was. The Leveller movement grew out of campaigns, first, for religious freedom, and, subsequently for the closely connected necessities of freedom of the press and of debate. The Levellers, like other mid-seventeenth-century radicals, were driven also by a burning sense of betrayal that for all the "blood and treasure" sacrificed in the civil war, it was the Parliament itself that was limiting these freedoms.[16] William Walwyn defended free trade as a natural right in 1652, but it was not at the forefront of his concerns for most of his life—religious freedom was clearly his first priority.[17] All this is to suggest that Leveller adherence to a free market was deduced from other elements of social life, rather than foundational to their views, within a context where the economic and social implications of market relations were already—long before the Industrial Revolution—less benevolent than Adam Smith or Professor Anderson believe.

Second, we need to complicate the notion of the market itself. The early modern market was not based on abstract notions of reciprocity, involving free and equal persons and straightforward monetary exchange. Market relationships were central to early modern England, but they operated on the basis of complex understandings of trust and credit, and credit here is a social and cultural concept not a merely technical process. As Craig Muldrew explains, early modern society encompassed "a market not just where things were bought and sold, but where trust was extended, or not extended, and where the social was defined as the need for, and the extent of such trust."[18] Actual money (that is coin or specie) was in short supply in early modern England, accounting was haphazard, and people often had only the broadest notion of their current economic position; the workings of society and economy depended on juggling debt and extending credit, forgoing or delaying repayments of debts, or rents. In receiving credit in this narrow sense, *credit* in its social meaning of esteem, reputation, or standing (to use some of the terms within Anderson's understanding of egalitarianism) was a vital advantage, and might help people of similar "real" economic capacity to flourish better in practice. The market was emphatically not an arena of abstract egalitarianism or individual equality, and well into the nineteenth century, "personal credit remained central to market relations, sometimes indistinct from and sometimes existing alongside gift relations."[19] The sharp contrast in Smith's thinking between market and gift transactions did not apply in practice.

Neither were the Levellers consistent in their approach to social and economic issues. In a time of social and economic upheaval, oppression and exploitation could be found in very different contexts, and the Levellers constructed a movement out of various, complex, even contradictory issues and groups. Once seen as "possessive individualists," the Levellers equally often projected a sense of collective and communal activism. Their pamphlets often denounced many injustices, as in *Londons Liberty in Chains Discovered*, which ranged from the sufferings of John Lilburne and his wife to political domination within the city corporation and the struggles of provincial merchants.[20] Levellers were not always committed to a free market based on private property rights in our modern sense, but often defended customary rights, as part of their resistance to the power and domination of the rich. Those large numbers of early modern households already largely dependent on wage labor could not survive without other sources of income—a small cottage garden, or various forms of nonmarketized, or not quite marketized customary communal rights: the right to "glean," to pick up the dropped corn at harvest, or to fatten a pig or graze a cow on common land. This involved differential rights over the same piece of property; it might be conceived of as specific to certain (private) individuals, but it was more properly a collective, multiple, layered concept of ownership. So the Levellers supported the "free miners" of Derbyshire who claimed the right, by ancient custom, to mine for lead wherever it was found against the increasing protests of landowners who claimed sole and absolute ownership of the surface land and all that was found beneath it; and they offered help to the small proprietors in the fens whose complex livelihoods of fishing, crafts, and farming were being destroyed by drainage projects.[21] All this may complicate but perhaps enrich the ways in which we look to the Levellers for experiments in egalitarianism and activism.

Third, and much more schematically than I would like, I want to raise some qualifications to the picture of the Levellers as a feminist movement. As Professor Anderson has shown, women were active Levellers; among individuals we can highlight Elizabeth Lilburne, Mary Overton, and Ellen Larner, and the radical religious separatist and author Katherine Chidley. The attack on a monarch whose rule was legitimated partly through patriarchalism had implications for gender hierarchies within the household, although most parliamentarians and republicans were very careful to limit these implications, most often through various versions of a separation between public or civil authority from the private world of the household. As Professor Anderson stressed, religious pluralism disrupted earthly hierarchies and challenged notions of sin and obedience: everyone should obey God before man, and men and women alike were equal before God. Leveller women insisted on their right to petition Parliament: "we knowing that for our encouragement and example, God hath wrought many deliverances for several nations from age to age, by the weak hand of women," and claimed an "equal share and interest with men in the commonwealth." But I am not convinced that Levellers as a movement thought that family power was monopolized by men; rather, I think they often fell back on a conception of society as made up of male-headed households, with women as valued but subordinate participants. John Lilburne referred to his loyal and long-suffering wife as the "weaker vessel," and Leveller rituals, like Leveller publications, presented the movement as a collectivity made up of various elements distinguished by place and by (I think) assumptions of natural inequality. In the funeral procession for Robert Lockyer, a Leveller sympathizer executed in May 1649 for his part in army mutinies, "citizens and women" and "youth and maids" followed the hearse in solemn but differentiated order. We remember again Rainborough's poorest "he" at Putney, the idea that servants and apprentices were included with their masters, and the fact that formal political rights for women as agents rather than as petitioners were never part of the Leveller agenda.[22] This view can be challenged but it is also worth remembering the classic arguments of feminist political philosophers that expansions of male political rights often prompted an intensification of arguments that women were unsuited by nature to political participation.[23] The problems for women and markets go beyond ignoring women's labor in the household, although that is one crucial aspect, as the lecture explains. More fundamentally, the difficulties are founded on the fact that, in the early modern case at least, the basic unit that competes in the market,[24] or aspires to political agency, is a household rather than an individual, and its head is normally, naturally (a word we need to highlight and challenge) assumed to be male.[25]

It is really exciting to see egalitarianism as about more than economic issues—to see it as a commitment to a broad enhancing of human capacities, enabling a fulfilling independence from the domination of others. I have responded to Professor Anderson's first lecture as a seventeenth-century historian, but I am also conscious of an upbringing within British social democratic or socialist traditions. Both combine to make me unconvinced that everything went wrong with the "Industrial Revolution"; seventeenth-century England was already a society where some half, at least, of the population, had little prospect of competing on equal terms in the market. Differential access to capital, credit, skill, training, time were all connected to wealth (which brought more advantage to its holders than "dominion" or "vanities"). I want to present a darker view of the potential of the seventeenth-century example, and I still think that economic inequality cannot be detached from the broader elements Professor Anderson has focused on.

Chapter 4

Market Rationalization

David Bromwich

Elizabeth Anderson's provocative discussion of the relationship between theories of political liberalism and market society asks a large question and has the probity to leave the answer open. The question concerns the party of equality that Europeans call the left and Americans think of roughly as the liberal side. How could this party have had so optimistic a start around 1640—when it identified the market with individual initiative, the energy of personal enterprise, a version of the career open to talents—yet by the end of the nineteenth century have come to view the market as an arrangement that suppresses equality and widens the distance between the poorest and the richest members of society?

Throughout her lectures, Anderson argues (in effect) that political theory should not stop at the door of the workplace. Supposing we share that belief, we still have to ask what prevented the new economic doctrine of the eighteenth century and the liberal political theory of the nineteenth from leading finally to acceptance of a democratic doctrine of self-government among men and women at work. Some reasons for the failure of the transition from the free market to full democracy may be found in the ideally abridged "freedom" that was first applied as a predicate to the marketplace alone. It is not clear how far it was ever conceived for adaptation to modern politics.

"What happened," Anderson asks, "between Smith and Marx to reverse the egalitarian assessment of market society?" She thinks it natural to be puzzled by the reversal, because "Smith, no less than Marx, reviled selfishness." That is true, but it tells us very little. One may denounce selfishness without embracing equality. Anyone who is not an apologist for sheer privilege and inherited wealth *must* deplore selfishness in order to gain a hearing. The parallel between Smith and Marx seems a lot weaker if we put aside "selfishness" and ask instead what Smith meant by "self-interest": an idea he made central to the economic morale and the moralized economics of several generations following his own. Even allowing for the correctives *The Wealth of Nations* prescribes against useless wealth and massive disparities of power, a reader of Smith can hardly avoid the conclusion that his idea of self-interest gives a pretext and an agreeable complexion to selfishness. Self-interest, as he interprets it, operates for the long-term good of society, and does so almost independent of the will of the interested party. It thereby circumvents less mechanistic and more volitionally exacting ideas of the common good. Under a system pervaded by self-interest, society is improved without anyone having to think about it. The progress will continue so long as we shun the wasteful deployment of middlemen and reckless ventures to engross private fortunes through monopoly.

Why does the machine work so well? Because, says Smith, we inhabit a world of goods—a world whose natural emanation and expression is an infinity of possible exchanges. We live in a world of goods that wants to be explored. It is as if all the commodities we might enjoy were a harvest-in-waiting, a second nature within society, intricately adapted to the desires and collaborative amenabilities of the human animal. Greed—a close relation of the warrior virtue and civic vice that Smith would have called pride or vainglory—on this understanding, becomes an aberration rather than an inseparable part of human nature with which a liberal theory of politics must somehow grapple. Almost all of us, Smith believes, would want, if we could, to improve our lives by adding convenience after convenience to our common world of man-made things. The commerce that comes with industrial capitalism will be useful and unsuperfluous. Also, the laborer in this system will have acquired, as Anderson tells us, the moral assets of "authority," "esteem," and "standing"—goods whose diffusion is necessary to democracy, though in earlier times they were known only to a fortunate elite.

Smith and Locke are the figures in modern political thought whom Anderson sifts for egalitarian intimations. How shall we add up their hints? Monopoly, for Smith, is inefficient and chokes invention. So far, he is certainly helpful to the critic of abuses in a capitalist system. But can we look to Smith for an argument against a multipurpose and endlessly diversified monopoly like Amazon or Google or the others that have arisen in our time? After all, these suppliers do satisfy our creaturely hunger for goods. They get their profits and our subsequent custom without suppressing a single desire for a single good. They constantly test our wishes and demands, and they run ahead of our conscious choices. Their success indicates that the machine of the market has changed in ways that Smith could not have anticipated.

Again, if we search for guidance from Locke on the relation between labor and property, we may be struck by the limited foresight his thinking offers. Anderson praises Locke's theory of government for its whole-length rejection of patriarchy, but how far does that take us on the path to equality in the society at large? The entrepreneur, says Locke, who mixes his labor with the land or with any piece of nature, and who thereby effects an improvement of some sort, rightly becomes the possessor of all he has worked on (provided that other lands or other fruits of nature are available to other people). Meanwhile, the harmless thriving individual who is not a member of the subspecies *appropriative man* is required to yield the right of enclosure and property to the energetic laborer. Market society, as Locke seems to have envisaged it, does not lead to equality between these two different tendencies that human nature has been known to pursue.

As for Thomas Paine—a radical democrat through and through and a believer in the market, too—he may belong to a different history. Paine began as a stay maker. He pictured literate self-respecting tradesmen like himself as the typical constituents of a town meeting. And he would have said of town meetings, as he did say of the provincial constitutions in America, that they are the grammar of the language of democracy. Paine's vision, however, was essentially political and only secondarily economic. It is true that a free market was a feature of democracy that Paine regarded as a natural concomitant of the rights of man. Still, the imperative pressure of his attack on monarchy and aristocracy comes from an idea of political liberty. It has little to do with an idea of supply and demand and collaborative labor such as we find in Smith and, to a lesser extent, in Locke.

But the underlying subject of Anderson's historical sketch is neither the liberal economic theory of Smith nor the political theory broadly shared by Locke, Paine, and Abraham Lincoln. What she asks us to examine is rather a pair of rival intuitions about the effects of modernization, and she has in mind chiefly modernization accomplished by means of the market. How can the earlier and happier intuition have proved so wrong? It may help to look closely at the famous sentence that concludes the first chapter of *The Wealth of Nations*. Smith there describes the household of a man of the middling sort, surrounded by all the goods that make his modest life comfortable: the utensils at his table, the glass in the window, the coals that heat the kitchen grate, the furniture, the bread, the beer, and so on. Think of all these things, says Smith, and you must realize that without such goods and the marvelous collaboration of their makers and suppliers, "the very meanest person in a civilized country could not be provided, even according to, what we very falsely imagine, the easy and simple manner in which he is commonly accommodated." Here then is the celebrated sentence:

> Compared, indeed, with the more extravagant luxury of the great, his accommodation must no doubt appear extremely simple and easy; and yet it may be true, perhaps, that the accommodation of an European prince does not always so much exceed that of an industrious and frugal peasant, as the accommodation of the latter exceeds that of many an African king, the absolute master of the lives and liberties of ten thousand naked savages.[1]

This presents an extraordinary image of the comfort and decency of modern society, seductive alike in its modesty and its grandeur. But we may ask: what is being compared to what?

A weaver, a tinker, a farrier, a costermonger, or even, some way up the social scale, a miller or a brewer in a small way of dealing, could think himself doing work intelligibly related to the work of a trader in spices and silks. All were rewarded for the production of goods whose value stemmed from artisanal training and extended practice; or they were rewarded for selling goods whose value they knew by experience, from a wide opportunity for comparisons. Was Smith therefore giving us an accurate picture? Did his society deserve the compliment he paid it? The European prince and the peasant are doubtless members of what Smith could suppose a market society, and in that society, the prince and the peasant are closer together (because of their access to market goods) than the African king is to the same peasant. On the other hand, the African king has *power*, and with his power, a fearlessness of misery, which is denied to the European peasant.

This difference—the difference between political power and market equality—I find underrated or insufficiently marked in Anderson's view of market society. But they were always distinct goods and they have remained distinct. In "the rise of masterless men" in the seventeenth century, Anderson discovers the germ of a spirit that tended toward democratic equality. As she describes them, these persons were invigorated by the new knowledge that they could become the makers of their own lives; among them were many nameless heroes whose ethic of individual conscience gave considerable impetus to the Puritan revolution. Being masterless, they found that they could ascend the social ladder, as they never could have done in the care of masters. This is a speculative area, of course, and one cannot be sure of causation or correlation. It makes sense that a new freedom for individual laborers should have gone hand-in-hand with the rise of a political theory that dispensed with arbitrary subordination and the rise of an economic theory that devalued the social bonds of feudalism. But how fortunate were the masterless men of the seventeenth century? How did they actually live? We know anyway that a different kind of masterless men began to be seen in the middle of the eighteenth century. These men were descending into masterless servitude.

The narrator of Oliver Goldsmith's poem "The Deserted Village"—published in 1770, six years before *The Wealth of Nations*—returns to the village in which he was brought up and finds it almost vacant. What caused the change? The industry soon to be celebrated by Smith, it seems, has also driven tradesmen and common citizens into lives of permanent displacement and destitution:

> Ill fares the land, to hastening ills a prey,
> Where wealth accumulates and men decay;
> Princes and lords may flourish or may fade;
> A breath can make them, as a breath has made;
> But a bold peasantry, their country's pride,
> When once destroyed, can never be supplied.[2]

Goldsmith goes on to speak of a lost England (in a memory derived also from his native Ireland), where "light labour" prevailed and imparted "just what life required." But to have a reasonable chance of happiness now, such ordinary labor has been forced to seek "a kinder shore."

In the narrative that follows, blending recollections of the village and anecdotes of its decay, the narrator comes upon a woman he remembers, a widow who lives now in a "nightly shed." He introduces us to the village preacher who was once freely sought out in his "modest mansion" for religious counsel and consolation; and to the schoolmaster, about whom all the village used to declare "how much he knew; / 'Twas certain he could write, and cypher too." This scholar served as the local historian—a function that the narrator himself now must take up. Goldsmith ends by adjuring himself to speak as the prophet of a departed way of life. His calling will be to memorialize the dead and tally the cost of the triumph of market society. So he warns us:

> That trade's proud empire hastes to swift decay,
> As ocean sweeps the laboured mole away;
> While self-dependent power can time defy,
> As rocks resist the billows and the sky.[3]

Notice that it is trade itself and not just "opulence" that has wrought the destruction; and trade, not only on the selfish mercantilist pattern that Smith so tellingly analyzed, but of the most energetic and prosperous kind. Goldsmith condemns the very idea of trade as the central meaning and justification of society. For trade uproots lives and turns ancient occupations obsolete. What we lose in the process is the very thing that the new political economy has promised: "self-dependent power."

In the wake of the depression of the 1930s, reflecting on an upheaval that by then had lasted almost two centuries, Karl Polanyi in *The Great Transformation* judged that there was always an imperfect fit between democracy and the vision of market society cherished by the classical economists:

> Labor, land, and money are essential elements of industry; they also must be organized in markets; in fact these markets form an absolutely vital part of the economic system. But labor, land, and money are obviously *not* commodities; the postulate that anything that is bought and sold must

have been produced for sale is emphatically untrue in regard to them. . . . Labor is only another name for a human activity which goes with life itself, which in its turn is not produced for sale but for entirely different reasons, nor can that activity be detached from the rest of life, be stored or mobilized; land is only another name for nature, which is not produced by man; actual money, finally, is merely a token of purchasing power which, as a rule, is not produced at all, but comes into being through the mechanism of banking or state finance. None of them is produced for sale. The commodity description of labor, land, and money is entirely fictitious.[4]

Yet this pleasing fiction, wrote Polanyi, guided the actual organization of modern markets for labor, land, and money in the nineteenth and the early twentieth century.

The transformation was well under way in the middle of the eighteenth century. By the time that Smith and Goldsmith wrote, the new system had begun to be the organizing principle of the entire society, "according to which no arrangement or behavior should be allowed to exist that might prevent the actual functioning of the market mechanism on the lines of the commodity fiction." But we have come to realize that society itself cannot ultimately survive in these conditions:

> For the alleged commodity "labor power" cannot be shoved about, used indiscriminately, or even left unused, without affecting also the human individual who happens to be the bearer of this peculiar commodity. In disposing of a man's labor power the system would, incidentally, dispose of the physical, psychological, and moral entity "man" attached to that tag. Robbed of the protective covering of cultural

institutions, human beings would perish from the effects of
social exposure; they would die as the victims of acute social
dislocation through vice, perversion, crime, and starvation.
Nature would be reduced to its elements, neighborhoods
and landscapes defiled, rivers polluted.[5]

We who have passed through the recession of 2000s have
come to know this truth almost as intimately as Polanyi when
he wrote in the early 1940s.

I conclude with a word about the three essential goods—
authority, esteem, and standing—whose value for democracy
makes a large part of the subject of Elizabeth Anderson's lectures. I prefer the plain word *power* to the subtler and more
elusive *authority*, and have noticed that Smith himself, in a passage quoted by Anderson, combines "power and authority"
so as to draw no sharp distinction between them. Ever since
the revolutions of the seventeenth century, any representative
of the left or the liberal side in politics has been compelled to
be jealous of political authority, or, to say it straight, political
power. This jealousy is a necessary and not a regrettable condition of political democracy. We ought to be jealous in the
sense that makes zeal a necessary root of jealousy and jealousy
itself a virtue. I am grateful to Elizabeth Anderson for having
given us an occasion to think closely again about the early modern theories of equality and freedom that rationalize but do not
justify our own market society.

Chapter 5

Help Wanted: Subordinates

Niko Kolodny

It's an honor to comment on Elizabeth Anderson's lectures—not least because I come to the task already strongly influenced by the article that contains their seeds, "What Is the Point of Equality?"[1] When that article appeared, in 1999, philosophical discussion of equality was at a dead end. On the one hand, those philosophers who thought that equality mattered had sealed themselves into a seemingly increasingly sterile debate about what sort of *stuff* we should be equalizing. On the other hand, many other philosophers doubted that equality did matter. It might matter whether the poor got more, and giving them more might, as a kind of by-product, close the gap between them and the rich. But surely the gap in stuff didn't matter in itself. After all, if it did, then instead of closing the gap by taking from the rich and giving to the poor, we might as well close it by taking from the rich and tossing in the ocean.

In a way that is truly rare in philosophy, Anderson's paper reoriented the debate.[2] What fundamentally mattered, she argued, were social *relations* of equality among people. If equalizing *stuff* mattered, it was because of how inequalities of stuff might affect such social relations. And what mattered really was *equality* in those relations. It wasn't as though my wife and I, married that year, could reduce our unstated concern for an egalitarian marriage to a concern that each spouse independently have as much of something as possible, with greater weights assigned to the spouse with less, should opportunities for redistribution arise, which would tend, as a kind of by-product, to equalize this something. That simply wasn't the right way to think about a marriage of equals.

So Anderson's work wrought an important change at least in philosophers' thinking about equality. And heightened concern, since 1999, about long-term trends toward certain forms of economic inequality has made her work only more timely. Yet, while I think that Anderson is onto something in turning our focus to social relations of equality, I struggle, as a committed partisan, to get clear about what exactly it is she's onto. It's easy enough to call to mind images of domineering masters and groveling servants. And these images make us, or at least Anderson and me, uneasy. But what is it in these images that disquiets us? Discretion? Hierarchy? And what alternative social arrangements, even in principle, could put us at ease? Law? Democracy? Anderson's lectures raise these questions once more.

What is Anderson's objection to too much of what, in her view, goes on in the contemporary workplace? It's not how much people are paid, or whether the job comes with health insurance or child care. It's not how boring, dangerous, or uncomfortable the work is. It's not whether people can count on keeping their job, or getting another one. Needless to say, she cares about these things. It's just that they're not her focus here. Her focus is instead the quasi-political relations of "government" between employers and employees within the firm. Although she defines "government" in terms of the issuing and enforcing of commands, this is actually too narrow for her purposes. Your boss isn't issuing or enforcing commands when he fires you for being too attractive or snoops in your inbox. While I'm not sure how to revise her definition, the rough idea is clear enough: The relations of employee to firm are somehow troublingly like the relations of subject to state, but without the liberal-democratic protections that might make the latter acceptable.

To throw Anderson's specific issue into relief, consider, as a kind of natural thought-experiment, the garment industry on the Lower East Side at the end of the nineteenth century. Some were employed in factories, while others (especially women, children, and those who refused to work on the Jewish Sabbath) did piecework from home.[3] All the same, the conditions at home in the tenements were hot, dark, chokingly cramped; the work was numbing and relentless; and the livelihood of a pieceworker was anything but secure. Anderson's focus is, roughly, how things, as bad as they were in the tenements, might have gotten *worse* had they gone to work in the factories—if, six days a week, they had to cross back and forth over the border into some capitalist's shirtwaist Lichtenstein.

But how does "government" make things worse? No doubt, it can be irksome to have your boss, copy of Frederick Taylor's *The Principles of Scientific Management* in hand, peering over your shoulder.[4] And it can be unpleasant to be restricted in the minutiae of when, where, and how you work—for example, not being free to put needle and thread down whenever nature calls. However, monitoring and restriction takes place even in the absence of "government." Even if you are a self-employed mime, or hairdresser, or hot-rivet-tosser, your every move will be carefully watched by your audience, or client, or hot-rivet-catcher. For that matter, even in the tenement, you may be tailed by a passive-aggressive, that's-not-how-you-do-it-but-far-be-it-from-me-to-interfere father-in-law. And all kinds of labor can be spoiled, or otherwise made more costly or less productive, unless the laborer can hold it in until an appropriate time. Granted, the need to monitor and restrict a given worker often derives from a production process that requires coordination with other workers. And, granted, such coordination would often not be feasible, human nature being what it is, without the "government" of the firm. All the same, the blame for the obnoxious monitoring and restricting seems to rest not with the "government" of the firm, but instead with the nature of the production process itself.

So what new evils does the "government" of the firm really add? Anderson's lecture suggests, to my mind, two main answers.

The first might be labeled "abuse of power"—or, better, "use of an unjustified power." Grant that there is a sound economic justification, of the kind pioneered by R. H. Coase, "The Nature of the Firm," for having firms.[5] At least when firms are complemented with other institutions, it works to everyone's benefit to have them. And to have firms is, in part, to give certain people certain powers over others within the firm. The concern is that, unless care is taken, in giving those people those *justified* powers, we also give them *unjustified* powers.

Some of these unjustified powers have no economic rationale at all, such as the power to monitor or restrict your employees in ways that don't make them more productive, or to fire them for not waxing your car. But I doubt that Anderson would leave it at that and concede that any power that improves the company's bottom line is thereby justified. Even powers that have an economic rationale can be unjustified if they are trumped by other values, which we are unwilling to compromise for economic gain. The powers may be degrading or inhumane, or may violate expectations that we associate with civil liberties, such as privacy or free speech. So, the trouble is that if we give the employer the justified power to fire a worker for slacking off, we risk also giving the employer the unjustified power to fire a worker for, say, not waxing his car. If we give employers the justified power to review work-related e-mail, we risk giving employers the unjustified power to review private e-mail stored in the same location. And so on.

The objection isn't simply to the package of work, compensation, and job security that is liable to result from the unjustified power. For example, the objection isn't merely that whereas in the tenement, you only had to sew on the buttons, now in factory, you have to sew on the buttons *and* wax some goy's horseless carriage—more work. The objection is also simply to being under the power of another person in a way that has no good justification. After all, particular abuses of power can be to the "victim's" benefit. Suppose your boss says: "Your slacking this morning was the last straw. The pink slip's in my outbox. But if you wax my car, I'll go and tear it up." That's arguably better than: "Your slacking this morning was the last straw. You're fired, case closed." At least the offer gives you the option to keep the job. (Compare when the blackmailer says, "You should thank me that I'm giving you the chance to hush this up, before I go to the press." There is a sense in which you really *should* thank him.) The objection isn't that the exercise of the unjustified power necessarily makes things worse for you.

It's rather that, while it's OK for other people to have power over your fate as a necessary part of a system that works to everyone's advantage, it's not OK for people to have power over your fate so that they, personally, can get their cars waxed.[6]

Suppose, however, that your boss wields only justified powers over you, powers justified by the company's bottom line, as constrained by the Bill of Rights. Still—and perhaps this is the heart of the matter for Anderson—you are "governed" by another person. Your boss still, well, *bosses* you.

But what's wrong about being governed by other people? I mean, to cut to the chase, we're all governed by the state. It issues and enforces commands, and wields vast power over our lives. This would be true even of the social democratic utopia of the sort that Anderson and I would favor, with its free day care, publicly financed elections, and frolicking sprites and elves. If it wouldn't be objectionable to be governed by such a state, why should it be objectionable to be governed by the firm? What's the difference?

Is the trouble, as Anderson sometimes suggests, being under the boss's *whim or discretion*—for example, his all-about-the-bottom-line hunches about how to deploy his workforce—whereas the state's commands are a matter of *rules or law*? I doubt it. The rules that govern life behind the counter at your local McDonald's might well be, in terms of their *form*, everything that Montesquieu, in *The Spirit of the Laws*, or Lon Fuller, in *The Morality of Law*, could wish for.[7] And why should laws be better than whims, in any event? Predictability can't be the answer. The vicissitudes of the market, to which the tenement pieceworker is subject, are at least as unpredictable as the whims of a boss. Perhaps the appeal of law, as opposed to whim, is that law is impersonal. To be ruled by law is not to be ruled by men. But surely this is an illusion. You only need the first three words of the U.S. Constitution to verify that it, no less than a McDonald's franchise agreement, was drawn up by people.

This takes us to what I think is the real issue, if there is one here: namely, *who* is responsible for the laws. The difference, as Anderson at other times suggests, is that at least our idealized state's laws are democratic, whereas McDonald's laws are oligarchic. First, at least to the extent that the state is realizing the aspirations of democracy, each of us has, at some fundamental level, an equal opportunity to determine what the state's laws are, or who will make them, whereas only a few of us get to approve the textbooks for Hamburger University. Second, although some will surely go on to have greater opportunity to make further determinations about the law, its application, and its enforcement, they do so as our delegates or agents. It's no easy thing to say what this relation of delegation requires. But presumably it requires, at least, that our delegates be accountable to us—something that Anderson stresses is rarely the case in the firm. The underlying concern, in other words, is that when the few, who aren't delegates, issue and enforce commands, or wield powers, to which the rest of us are subject, that seems incompatible with relations of equality between them and us—the sorts of relations of equality highlighted in Anderson's watershed 1999 article.

Some may think that this only pushes the problem back: "If there's a problem about being under an alien *will*, then why isn't there a problem about being under the *democratic* will?" This complaint seems appropriate if you see the problem as one of individual freedom; if the ideal is a kind of personal insulation from any "alien will." But it makes less sense if you see the problem rather as one about *equality*: your symmetrical standing with others. Granted, simply in virtue of being subject to the state's decisions, you're still exposed to a will that—no matter what Jean-Jacques Rousseau, in the *Social Contract*, might have told you—is not really your own.[8] But if the state is realizing the democratic aspiration, then you're not, simply in virtue of being subject to its decisions, subordinated to any other individual. There's no one in society to whom you can point and say, "Because she had more opportunity to influence the decision than I have, I am, merely in being subjected to the decision, subordinated to her." To be sure, this is no guarantee the decisions will treat you well. But there's no guarantee the monsoon winds, or the market for piecework, will treat you well either. Our question, again, is what's especially problematic about being under the governance of another person, after we have controlled for things that you can suffer even without that yoke.

So, I've tried to tease out two main suggestions about why the "government" that the firm involves might be distinctively objectionable. There's a worry about some wielding powers over others that lack an economic rationale, or an economic rationale sufficient to trump the basic rights at stake. There's a worry about being subordinated, or put in relations of inferiority, to other individuals. But how worrying are these worries about the firm?

The rhetorical tendency of Anderson's lecture is to equate the situation of the employee with the situation of the political subject, and so to demand for the employee everything that we would demand for the subject. But surely she thinks that the situation of the employee is different, and that the firm gets a pass on some things a state wouldn't. I doubt that she would insist on workplace democracy, as she would for state democracy. It scarcely seems possible for the firm to respect all of our civil rights. Just take free choice of occupation itself. I shouldn't lose U.S. citizenship if I choose to be a dog walker rather than a mouse impersonator, but surely Chuck E. Cheese's can exile me for that choice.

So, what puts the brakes on the rhetorical momentum toward full equivalence? What makes acceptable from the firm what would be unacceptable from the state: including oligarchy and economically productive violations of what would otherwise be civil liberties? Is it that the worst that Chuck E. Cheese's can do is exile me? That exile from Chuck E. Cheese's isn't, after all, as costly? That I consented to the terms of employment in a way in which I didn't consent to U.S. citizenship? That the firm itself is regulated by a legal order that I have equal opportunity to influence: that whatever hierarchy the firm involves is ultimately controlled from a standpoint of equality? At one point or another in the lecture, Anderson minimizes each of these differences.[9] My consent to *this* firm matters little, for example, given that—as would be true even in our utopia—I must consent to *some* firm. Yet ultimately, she must fall back on some or all of these differences. Once we do stress these differences, once we do apply these brakes, how close to the state does the firm end up? And how seriously should we then be troubled that our rights as employees are not like our rights as citizens?

I'm not sure what the answers are. But I am sure that we're in Anderson's debt for spurring us to ask the questions.

Chapter 6

Work Isn't So Bad after All

Tyler Cowen

I am very much a fan of Elizabeth Anderson's attempts to synthesize philosophy and economics, but on the topic of her Tanner entry my views diverge from hers. I see the economics differently, and when it comes to the moral philosophy, I would put the practical trade-offs front and center of the argument, and allow them to shape the philosophy, rather than presenting them as an afterthought.

I won't summarize her views, but I will pull out one phrase that is central to her piece—namely, she refers early on to "communist dictatorships in our midst." These communist dictators are, in her account, private business firms. That description may be deliberately hyperbolic, but nonetheless it reflects her attitude that capitalist companies exercise a kind of unaccountable, nondemocratic power over the lives of their workers, in a manner that she considers to be extremely morally objectionable.

As an individual who chose an academic job to maximize some dimensions of my personal freedom, I sympathize with parts of this portrait. Still, I would stress some very different facts and features of the employment relationship.

For instance, I don't worry so much about the dictatorial power of companies if the costs of worker exit are relatively low. To be sure, many workers grow attached to their current firms—for instance, they may have friends there, a good relationship with the boss, and a preferred commute. Still, the most likely scenario is that such perks accumulate and the wages of these workers fail to advance, due to employer financial exploitation. That may be a problem, but it is hardly the dilemma outlined by Anderson, which has more to do with insufficient worker freedom.

Many corporate critics, including Anderson at the tail end of her piece, postulate the existence of "monopsony"—namely, that a single company has a good deal of market power of the workers it employs. I am worried she, like others, doesn't offer much evidence to back up her portrait, save for one footnote to an adequate but not very influential book. In contrast to her treatment, the best study I know finds that Walmart—the largest private sector employer in America—does not have significant monopsony power in most regions, some parts of the rural south and center excepted. The monopsony model of employment has attracted some attention—much of it from Princeton, I might add—but most economists assign it only a secondary status in explaining labor markets. And without monopsony, we are back to the idea of exit as helping to enforce a lot of worker freedoms.[1]

More generally, it is well recognized that larger firms pay workers considerably more than do smaller firms. Strictly speaking, this is not incompatible with a monopsony model (for example, market power may cause wages to be bid up as a large firm hires more), but it is a very different reality than what Anderson communicates. Note also that larger firms tend to be more tolerant of employee personal tastes than are smaller firms. For instance, the local auto parts store, with its "ol' boys network," may be reluctant to hire gays and minorities, but McDonald's has policies favoring tolerance, in part to protect the broader reputation of the company with a wide variety of customers. I would put those facts front and center of any account of the modern business corporation, but Anderson seems to be offering a largely negative portrait of how business economies of scale interact with the personal freedoms of workers.[2]

It is worth noting that the monopsony model does not itself predict workers will enjoy less freedom or fewer perks in the workplace. This sounds counterintuitive, as we associate monopsony with lower bargaining power for workers and thus inferior working conditions. But rest assured, I am offering the correct reading of theory. Some time ago economists realized that product monopoly does not predict lower product quality, as profits may be maximized more readily at a higher product quality level than a lower product quality level (for example, you might rather monopolize diamonds than cheaper stones). An analogous proposition holds for monopsony—namely, that employers may improve workplace freedoms so that they may lower worker wages all the more. And this isn't just a theoretical possibility, it seems in the real world, we see employers catering to the job-quality preferences of the incumbents, rather than the marginal new hires, really quite often. Or consider an employer who would like to lure in more workers, but without bidding up wages for all workers as a clumsy monopsonistic giant is likely to do. Offering employees selective workplace freedoms is one possible way to "wage discriminate" and increase company profits. I'm not saying it has to work out this way, but it easily can.[3]

So even if the monopsony assumptions are descriptively relevant, they don't connect very easily to the notion of an absence of workplace freedom.

That all said, I readily grant the costs of exiting many jobs are too high, and I would suggest focusing on the very concrete question of how public policy could lower these costs. Health insurance, retirement benefits, and immigration status are often too closely tied to particular jobs, largely as artifacts of regulation and tax law. For instance, we should level the playing field for employer-supplied health insurance (ACA attempts to do this partly with its "Cadillac tax"), and we should make immigration status for many workers less tied to remaining at particular jobs. The reality is that many cases of worker dependence on corporations spring from bad government decisions rather than directly from markets or the nature of the corporate employment relationship.

It's also worth challenging some of the fundamental premises of Anderson's argument. This may sound counterintuitive or even horrible to many people, but the economist will ask whether workers might not enjoy "too much" tolerance and freedom in the workplace, at least relative to feasible alternatives. For every benefit, there is a trade-off, and the broader employment offer as a whole might involve too little cash and too much freedom and tolerance. To oversimplify a bit, at the margin, an employer can pay workers more either with money or with freedom and tolerance, which we more generally can label as perks. Money is taxed, often at fairly high rates, whereas the workplace perks are not; that's one reason why a lot of Swedish offices are pretty nice. It's simple economics to see that, as a result, the job ends up with too many perks and not enough pay, relative to a social optimum. I doubt if our response to this distorting tax wedge, which can be significant, should be to increase the perks of the workers rather than focusing on increasing their pay.

Arguably individual preferences are not morally sacrosanct here, as philosophical notions of dignity and the like may intervene, as Amartya Sen and others—including Elizabeth Anderson—have argued in other contexts. Fair enough, but let's emphasize that individual preferences probably are pushing fairly strongly in the direction of higher pay rather than higher perks, given the initial tax distortion.[4]

I believe also that a business usually should have the right to fire a worker for Facebook postings or other forms of "outside the workplace" activity. For a start, a lot of workers put racist, sexist, or otherwise discomforting comments and photos into their Facebook pages. When employers fire them, very often it is to protect some notion of *the freedom of the other workers*. As I read Anderson, usually she frames the issues in terms of the employer versus the workers. But through markets, employers very often are internalizing the preferences of the workers as a whole. The question of workplace freedom often boils down to one set of the workers against another. In that setting, allowing for a lot of apparently arbitrary firing decisions on net may support rather than oppose worker autonomy.

Overall, I find the perspective of the employer and also the perspective of the customer to be lacking in her essay, as employers are mostly viewed as controlling workers or at least trying to do so. There is a pretty simple law and economics story that employer discretion is required because a lot of employee transgressions and misbehaviors cannot be specified in easily contractible or legally enforceable ways. At the margins, that employer discretion leads to abuses, some of which are documented in Anderson's piece. But those abuses are relatively few in number, and *the gains for workers and customers from the firing discretion*—not just the gains for bosses—outweigh those costs. Maybe this perspective is too simple, but Anderson never rebuts it. The proffered instances of employer abuse are presented as a *prima facie* argument against current arrangements, without a sufficient look at the offsetting benefits of that discretion. Furthermore, we are never told how many such cases of arbitrary firings have occurred or how high their human costs have been. I do not see the evidence that suggests such events are a major concern of the American public.

Economists in fact have a pretty good but not perfect explanation of why employers often have so much discretionary authority over workers. The employers (often, not always) have a more unique contribution to the value of the capital goods, and thus they own the property rights to that capital, as outlined by Sanford Grossman, Oliver Hart, and John Moore in a series of papers.[5] Ultimately, most workers benefit from this arrangement, if only in their role as consumers; most people don't want their co-workers in charge of the ultimate disposition of the capital goods. There is plenty of evidence that workers require some degree of external control, and often themselves recognize this as such.[6]

That said, I do participate in a worker-owned firm myself— namely, my Marginal Revolution blog with Alex Tabarrok, which is owned by the two of us. As the main writers, we're the ones who add the value, and capital costs are very low, and so this organizational form makes sense and indeed is predicted by economics. Otherwise, I let my university pay me and, at the same time, tell me I cannot have obscene material on my computer, or perhaps I cannot blog or tweet very offensive remarks (as defined by them), as a condition of continued employment. I'm happy with that mix, and in return I don't have to wear a suit and tie to work.

I'm not trying to argue that current arrangements represent an ideal for everyone or even most people. But to evaluate such questions, we need to build the trade-offs into our moral theory at an earlier level than what I see Anderson doing.

Overall, corporate impositions on worker dignity aren't nearly as great as Anderson makes them out to be. Large numbers of employers go out of their way to make their companies *sources* of worker dignity, precisely because workers and potential workers value such freedoms and protections. The more your company is viewed positively, the easier it is to recruit talented workers. I don't see that perspective getting enough play. A lot of people don't like working at home because they receive too much pleasure and fulfillment from their workplaces, even though some conformity is expected. It is also well known that unemployment has major negative effects on happiness and health, far beyond what the lost income otherwise would induce. Does this not indicate that workplaces, overall, are significant sources of human dignity and fulfillment in today's capitalist world? I think so, yet Anderson never rebuts or considers this side of the ledger. The desire to attract and keep talent is the single biggest reason why companies try to create pleasant and tolerant atmospheres for their workers, and why it is rare for businesses to fire workers for their political views or their (nondestructive) off-premises activities.

The contrast between business governance over workers and political "rule of law" is a potentially misleading one. I would note that under today's American "rule of law," if interpreted literally, the average American commits about three felonies each day (for instance, throwing out junk mail addressed to somebody else is a federal crime punishable with up to five years in prison).[7] Of course, most of us get off scot-free for these and many other crimes. I do think we should clear away many of these laws, but in the meantime they reflect a broader point: just about all workable systems rely on embedded incentives to make them tolerable. In this case, there is very little incentive to prosecute each American for three felonies each day. I am thus uncomfortable seeing arbitrary corporate governance juxtaposed against a supposed objective or neutral ideal of the rule of law, because the latter does not in fact exist and it is not what protects our political liberties in practice.

Perhaps most of all, I find that a discussion of the alternatives to current arrangements needs to come at the center of the analysis, as the key questions are fundamentally comparative ones. I would ask for a closer look at company bargains with labor unions, co-ops owned and run by their workers, and worker-managed firms. Overall, the literature shows that these structures do not offer significantly greater freedom for workers, at least not in the sense that Anderson describes. One reason is that these organizational structures often are less efficient, and that interferes with their ability to give workers a better deal. Another mechanism is that when workers can get a better deal, they often prefer to take cash rather than extra freedoms or perks. Different organizational forms therefore do not seem to be a significant answer to the problems of workplace freedom, nor are unions.

In fact, there are some reasons why labor-managed firms may give their workers *less* personal freedom. The old-style investment banking and legal partnerships expected their owner-members to adhere to some fairly strict social and professional codes, even outside the workplace. More generally, when workers are motivated to monitor each other, through the holding of equity shares, monitoring becomes easier and so corporations engage in more of it. Again, the main issue is not controlling bosses versus freedom-seeking workers.[8]

If there is a major problem that firms impose on workers, it is when they prematurely or mistakenly "liberate" them from the oppression of the workplace. Of course, I am talking about unemployment. Most economists agree that, from a social point of view, firms are too willing to lay off workers and too reluctant to cut their nominal wages as a way of keeping workers on board and making ends meet. And if you look at labor-managed firms, the evidence bears out this hypothesis. When workers have a say in governance, employment tends to be more stable and wages tend to be more volatile.[9] In other words, the real problem with bosses is that they are too willing to give up "control" over their workers.

Anderson mentions the German codetermination model, whereby workers sit on the boards of corporations. The best study I know indicates that this organizational form costs about 26 percent of shareholder value because of lower productivity,[10] and furthermore a lot of that burden is born by consumers, who of course are mostly workers in another guise. And that result is for Germany, the country where this organizational model probably has been most successful. Furthermore, the codetermination model works best for midlevel manufacturing firms—which are prevalent in Germany—but does not generalize as easily to the service sector, where most workers may have less of a stake in the long-run interests of the firm.

In sum, I think Anderson's portrait is too negative toward business, too negative toward individual freedom as enjoyed in corporate workplaces, and too unwilling to confront the relevant trade-offs square on. The good news is that even the nonacademics among us do not toil under the supervision of communist dictators.

Response

Chapter 7

Reply to Commentators

Elizabeth Anderson

I am grateful to receive such thoughtful responses from my commentators, reflecting four different disciplines. This diversity is essential for coming to grips with the central problem I raise in my lectures—the critique of an ideology that misrepresents the situation of workers in the economy, and that is thereby unable either to appreciate their complaints or to generate and properly evaluate possible remedies. Ann Hughes, a historian of seventeenth-century England, and David Bromwich, a scholar of English literature and historian of ideas of the eighteenth century, helpfully remind us of those who lost out in the transition to market society even before the Industrial Revolution. They raise important questions about the ability of the early pro-market ideology to address the problems that market society generated at the time it was promulgated. Niko Kolodny, a philosopher, presses me to explain more fully what is objectionable about being subject to the arbitrary power of another. Tyler Cowen, an economist, stresses the need to weigh the costs and benefits of different workplace governance regimes. All of these perspectives deserve more discussion than I have space to offer here. I thank them all for raising their concerns, and wish my replies to be taken in the spirit of continuing the investigation of these issues, rather than as final answers.

The Divide between Pre– and Post–Industrial Revolution Pro-Market Theory

It is difficult to recover what early egalitarian pro-market thinkers believed, because our understanding of pro-market ideology is so profoundly shaped by what it became in the nineteenth century, in the hands of laissez-faire ideologues and neoclassical economists. The later ideology included several controversial positions: support for the commodification of labor, notwithstanding its negative consequences for workers' capacities and social standing; neglect of, or support for, the distributive consequences of markets, even when they concentrate their negative effects on vulnerable and disadvantaged groups; support for a property regime in which the income from land and capital accrues exclusively to their individual owners; a narrow focus on efficiency, economic growth, consumer satisfaction, and profits as the sole criteria for evaluating markets; a belief that the economy can be analyzed as a system of self-regulating free markets, operating by their own mechanical laws in isolation from the rest of society, and that factor markets can be analyzed just like consumer markets; and a belief that a system in which individuals act solely for their self-interest will, by the laws of the market, produce benign outcomes for society at large. My early pro-market thinkers, Locke and Smith included, believed in *none* of these things.[1]

The difficulty is compounded by the fact that the predictions early egalitarian pro-market thinkers made about the effects on workers of freeing up markets turned out to be mistaken. It is all too easy to suppose that, because they supported free markets, they must have endorsed the actual outcomes they ultimately produced. Yet the Industrial Revolution effected a great *reversal* in the expected outcomes of a broadly free market regime. The ideology that arose to rationalize these outcomes ignored most of the criteria my early thinkers used to evaluate markets. Hence, to grasp what my early pro-market thinkers believed, we must take care not to project mid- to late-nineteenth-century laissez-faire doctrine on to them. With these precautions in mind, let us consider the comments of Ann Hughes and David Bromwich.

Hughes and Bromwich stress that, while the rise of market society improved the condition of many masterless men in the seventeenth and eighteenth centuries, it delivered miserable poverty and desperate insecurity to many others. The enclosure movement deprived many of access to land, leading them to seek wage labor not because they preferred it to their previous mode of existence, but because they were forced to resort to it, having been deprived of their previous, preferred way of life. Many lacked access even to steady wage labor and had to obtain their subsistence by cobbling together a set of even more marginal strategies—a bit of putting out, poaching from forests, occasional day or itinerant labor, poor relief, private charity, and so forth. Bromwich correctly notes that shifts in trade, too, devastated whole communities before the Industrial Revolution, with effects movingly depicted by Oliver

Goldsmith in 1770. Hughes and Bromwich suggest that the timing of these developments, which took place long before the Industrial Revolution, casts doubt on my argument: I can't say that everything went wrong with market society only with the Industrial Revolution, given the ways it was already harming workers long before.

I stress that my aim in these lectures is not to offer an assessment of market society at that time. Rather, I aim to understand and assess an evolving market-friendly *ideology* that emerged before the Industrial Revolution. My argument is not that the rise of market society was all good for workers until the Industrial Revolution. It is that the Industrial Revolution decisively undermined the *model* early egalitarians promoted, of how a market society, *with appropriate reforms*, could liberate workers. Their ideology did not simply endorse all the changes that were taking place in their times. They were troubled by the emerging wage labor system, and of the immiseration and stultification suffered by those subjected to it and to even worse conditions, such as slavery and unemployment. Ideologies do not simply describe and evaluate what exists. They promote ideals yet to be realized, diagnose the obstacles in the way, and suggest ways to remove those obstacles.

The ultimate ideal of this early market-friendly ideology was not wage labor, but self-employment. Pro-market thinkers from the Levellers through Lincoln diagnosed the obstacles to realizing this ideal as stemming from a corrupt system by which the state unjustly favored the powerful—the lords and the court, monopolist traders and manufacturers, manipulative financiers and bond traders, idle *rentiers*, parasitic occupants of state sinecures, slaveowners—at the expense of workers, who were actually or potentially self-employed. They argued that the miseries market society was then inflicting on the downtrodden could be addressed by breaking up monopolies, opening up opportunities to trade to all workers, freeing workers from involuntary servitude, eliminating state cronyism, imperialism, and the regressive taxes needed to fund it—in short, by freeing up markets and ending forms of state regulation that rigged the system in favor of the rich and powerful. By contrast, they approved of state action that favored workers. Even Smith, the supposed paragon of laissez-faire ideology, argued that whenever a regulation of "the differences between masters and their workmen . . . is in favour of the workmen, it is always just and equitable."[2]

Consider pro-market views of credit and debt in this light. Hughes observes that the market/gift distinction was blurred in seventeenth-century credit relations. The scarcity of specie put borrowers in a form of indebtedness to creditors that often could not be discharged by cash payment. An element of subordination, of duties to render higher respect and services in kind, often accompanied receipt of a loan. But pro-market thinkers did not simply approve of credit relations as they existed at the time. They anticipated a better order to come by heightening the cash nexus: far better to owe mere cash to a creditor than to suffer debt peonage or bondage. Bankruptcy law, a great invention of the emerging capitalist order, enabled discharge of an insolvent's debts with the chance to start anew. This was a vastly superior prospect to peonage or debtor's prison.[3]

Property rights, too, were changing in this period. Hughes and Bromwich note the catastrophe brought on the poor by enclosures. The Levellers defended the customary rights of the poor to the commons and to glean from property owned by landlords, rather than the emerging regime, which concentrated exclusive rights in single owners.[4] Customary rights might seem "anti-market" insofar as they enabled the poor to avoid resort to wage labor. Yet this is consistent with my point that the early pro-market view did not aim to promote the commodification of labor. Rather, they hoped that with the right reforms, the emerging market order would liberate people from servitude, including wage labor, rendering it—in Lincoln's most optimistic vision—at most as only a temporary stage of life. Among these reforms included massive *assaults* on what were then considered inviolable rights of property, including primogeniture, entail, chartered monopolies, and slavery. Paine, too, with his revolutionary proposal for social insurance funded through an inheritance tax, attacked the idea that property owners were entitled to monopolize all the income from their property: rather, landowners owed a rent to everyone else in society, payable upon their deaths.

The early pro-market thinkers I discuss were not blind to the fact that the emerging market order worsened conditions for many workers, and that entry into labor markets was often forced, not voluntary. They hoped, however, that an assault on "corruption"—on the ways the state rigged the rules of markets and property in favor of the rich and powerful at the expense of ordinary workers—along with pro-worker reforms, would enable market society to benefit all, in large part by empowering people to rise from a state in which they labored for others to one in which they worked for themselves. The pro-worker reforms they proposed beyond anti-corruption measures varied. Smith advocated state-funded education for workers.[5] Paine proposed a comprehensive system of social insurance and stakeholder grants for young adults. Lincoln won passage of the Homestead Act of 1862, which handed out free land in the territories to anyone who would work it. All opposed slavery and involuntary servitude.[6]

They turned out to be mistaken. Eliminating corruption, abolishing state-established monopolies and involuntary servitude, reforming property, and so forth were not enough to deliver what the early pro-market ideology promised. Smith's central premise, that economies of scale are negligible, so that free markets would allocate land and capital to the self-employed worker, was dashed by the Industrial Revolution.[7] Locke's and Lincoln's central premise, that virtually unlimited amounts of free land would always be available to workers, was doomed by population growth and the closure of the American frontier.

In addition, even had all of their predictions been realized, their egalitarian agenda was largely limited to white men. Notwithstanding their feminist sympathies, neither the Levellers (as Hughes notes) nor Paine developed a plausible set of reforms addressed to women. Smith and Lincoln neglected the subjection of women altogether. None came fully to grips with the evils of racism against blacks and indigenous peoples.

It is easy to see the flaws of an ideology in hindsight. It is much harder to appreciate its promise at the time it was developed. I argue *not* that the early pro-market theorists were correct, but that they had good reasons to believe at the time that making markets *more free*, along with other reforms, would liberate working people. In certain important respects, their agenda was right. Who would prefer to return to the days of primogeniture, merchant monopolies, serfdom, slavery, and debtor's prison? Paine's arguments for comprehensive social insurance, and Smith's for state-funded education, have been vindicated as well. But my thinkers offered an inadequate answer to the problems suffered by wage laborers, because they mistakenly believed that, with pro-market reforms, nearly all would escape that condition. They can hardly be blamed for failing to anticipate the Industrial Revolution and the resulting inability of their reform agenda to address the problems faced by workers who, to paraphrase Lincoln, were fixed in the condition of a wage laborer for life.

Thus, I take exception to Bromwich's conclusion that the early thinkers I discuss "rationalize but do not justify our own market society." They do not even rationalize it, since their hopeful model of market society represented wage labor as a minor and temporary resort for workers, rather than the central institution it is for the vast majority of workers in today's market societies. The earlier thinkers are less to blame for vesting their hopes in an ideal that was destroyed by unforeseeable changes, than its current purveyors are for promulgating it in a world it does not remotely describe, either currently or in prospect. That is the error I seek to correct in my second lecture.

What's Wrong with Subjection to Another's Private Government?

Niko Kolodny asks, "what's especially problematic about being under the governance of another person, after we have controlled for things that you can suffer even without that yoke?" I stress that the focus of my lectures is not government as such. This is inescapable in many domains, not just with respect to the state. In the workplace, too, organizations with some kind of internal hierarchy have proven indispensable for producing numerous complex goods. That is the lesson of the Industrial Revolution. My focus is *private government*—arbitrary, unaccountable authority. Against Kolodny, I would not set aside the harms people can suffer from arbitrary, unaccountable government that can also be brought about by other means. But

I embrace his view that I have two fundamental objections to private government. First, it makes those subject to it vulnerable to unjustified and abusive forms of power—beyond whatever legitimate authority employers have. Second, private government subjects people to social relations of inequality. What remains to be explained is, what's so bad about occupying the inferior position in an unequal social relation?[8] Let us consider the three dimensions of inequality—authority, standing, and esteem—in turn.

Kolodny argues that subjection to the authority of a taskmaster is no more vexing than subjection to tight natural constraints inherent in the production process. The pieceworker forced to adopt a relentless pace of work at home to earn enough to survive suffers just as much as the factory worker ordered to adopt a similarly relentless pace by her boss.[9] I disagree. To see the difference authority makes, consider the one-day strike of Skylab astronauts on December 28, 1973. Days before the strike,

NASA began sending extremely specific instructions about minute-by-minute tasks for the astronauts to accomplish.... They tried to keep up for two weeks but found themselves falling behind, as there was no room in the schedule for the natural delays that happen at work. Moreover, they were exhausted with these 16-hour days. When they fell behind, NASA began demanding less sleep and working through their meal breaks. So the astronauts began to complain to Mission Control. But NASA's response was that they were whining.... [Mission Commander Gerry] Carr and his crew demanded a day off. NASA refused. So Carr simply shut off the radio and the astronauts took the day off they wanted.... After the 1-day strike, NASA finally came to terms with the astronauts. The next day, December 29,

NASA agreed to quit micromanaging the astronauts, allowed them to take their full meal breaks, and just send them a list of tasks for the day and let them figure out how to get it done. You know, treat them like adults. And it worked. All the projects got done before the mission ended.[10]

Exercising autonomy—directing oneself in tasks, no matter how exacting and relentless they are—is no ordinary good. It is a basic human need. No production process is *inherently* so constrained as to eliminate all exercise of autonomy. Elimination of room for autonomy is the product of social design, not nature. It is not merely "unpleasant" to be denied a rest break when one needs it. When some authority denies it (as opposed to when some natural constraint prevents it), the restriction demeans one's agency. Having a genuine say in how one's work is directed, even when one must adjust to the claims of others, as in a collectively governed workplace, and even when one doesn't get one's way, still is an exercise of autonomy in the decision-making process, if not the outcome.

Now consider inequalities of standing and esteem. The two are closely related. Let's peek inside Amazon warehouses to see how the company treats its employees and temps. The pace of work is unremitting. Workers are reprimanded for "time theft" when they pause to catch their breath after an especially difficult job.[11] They are subjected to ever-increasing quotas, constantly yelled at for not making their quotas, threatened daily with discharge, and eventually fired when the required pace gets too high for them to meet—a fate of the vast majority of Amazon's hires. But not before they suffer injury on the job: workers have to get on hands and knees hundreds of times per day, a practice that leaves few unscathed. Amazon forces them to sign papers affirming that their injuries are not work-related, or they are given demerits that can lead to discharge. In 2011, at its Allentown, Pennsylvania, warehouse, Amazon allowed the indoor heat index to rise to 102 degrees. When employees asked to open the loading doors to let air circulate—a common practice at other warehouses—Amazon refused, claiming this would lead to employee theft. Instead, it parked ambulances outside, waiting for employees to collapse from heat stroke. When they did, they would be given demerits for missing work, and fired if they accumulated too many. Amazon didn't care, because regional unemployment was high, and they had hundreds of applicants to replace the fallen workers. Other warehouses are not so brutal: they are ventilated, install ergonomic equipment, and have a more manageable pace.[12] But Amazon refuses to take workers' complaints seriously. They are accused of being "selfish" for complaining, and told their only concern should be taking care of the customer.[13]

This is a paradigm of unequal standing: workers' interests count for nothing in Amazon's eyes. Only the customers' interests—and its own, which it asserts in hiding behind its customers—count.[14] The issue here isn't only that these conditions impair workers' health. In some circumstances, such as firefighting, exposure to dangerous conditions is unavoidable. The issue is inequality: Amazon treats workers' vital interests as of no account, in comparison with its own and its customers' relatively trifling interests. Its sickening working conditions, unlike the firefighters', are gratuitously imposed. This inequality inflicts an expressive injury on the workers, over and above the material injury of illness. Adam Smith understood this point:

> What chiefly enrages us against the man who injures or insults us, is the little account which he seems to make of us, the unreasonable preference which he gives to himself

above us, and that absurd self–love, by which he seems to imagine, that other people may be sacrificed at any time, to his conveniency or his humour. The glaring impropriety of this conduct, the gross insolence and injustice which it seems to involve in it, often shock and exasperate us more than all the mischief which we have suffered.[15]

Private government at work embeds inequalities in authority, standing, and esteem in the organizations upon which people depend for their livelihood. Those consigned to the status of wage worker for life have no real way out: while they can quit any given employer, often at great cost and risk, they cannot opt out of the wage labor system that structurally degrades and demeans them.

Kolodny rejects the rule of law as an illusion: all laws are made by people. Quite right, but this does not mean that the rule of law does not constrain people. And the point of the rule of law is to constrain the governors, not the governed.[16] To have to follow due process in making and enforcing laws, and in applying sanctions, provides vital protections against abuses of governors' discretionary power. It thereby gives those subject to the law a structural standing and respectability that they would otherwise lack. Thus, I do not endorse Kolodny's thought that all that matters is who makes the decisions. Even a direct democracy with majority voting would need to follow rule of law constraints to avoid degenerating into unjust rule.

Kolodny wonders, given the analogy I draw between state and workplace governance, why I don't simply endorse full workplace democracy. My fundamental reason is pragmatism: there are enough disanalogies between state and workplace governance that our experiences with democratic states do not give us enough information about what arrangements are likely to make sense for the workplace. In most workplaces, employees' activities need to be closely coordinated around both means and ends. Nothing close to that level of coordination among citizens is required to enable liberal states to supply public goods. Furthermore, the traditional model of workplace democracy assumed that workers would own the firm. Worker ownership is far out of reach for most firms, given the size of capital investment needed. It would be imprudent to advise most workers to invest all their savings in their workplace even if they could thereby own them. If owners are distinct from workers, workplace governance will also have to be made accountable to owners to ensure that their investment is not squandered. Finally, as I note in my second lecture, the experiments with workplace democracy that have been undertaken suggest that designing a viable democratic system of workplace governance is challenging: workers with heterogeneous interests have a hard time agreeing to a common constitution.

A priori arguments cannot settle what a just constitution of workplace governance would look like. It is possible that different types of workplace will best operate under different constitutions. We need to experiment to learn the costs and benefits of different forms of workplace governance. The main point I have argued in these lectures is that the problem of workplace governance needs to be put on the table for what it is: a problem of *government*, not of markets or "freedom of contract."

How Should We Evaluate the Constitution of Workplace Government?

Tyler Cowen raises some fundamental questions about the grounds for evaluating the constitution of workplace governance. To address them, I need to clarify the argument of my lectures. At points, Cowen interprets me as objecting to large-scale workplaces, and to the existence of authority within such workplaces. Had I endorsed the early pro-market ideology that I discuss in Lecture 1, I would object. But the point of my lectures is ideology *critique*, in two parts. In Lecture 1, I argue that the ideal of a free society of equals based on universal self-employment failed in its own terms, due to its dependence on patriarchal appropriation of women's labor and racist appropriation of Native American lands. The ideal was also doomed by the vast economies of scale brought about by the Industrial Revolution. In Lecture 2, I criticize the *legacies* of that ideal in contemporary American public discourse. These legacies include the ideas that all state regulation of the economy is an infringement on individual liberty, that the state is the only form of government, that our basic choices with respect to organizing production are between the state and the market, that individuals are free from control and authority in "the private sector," that the organization of work is a product of free contracts between workers and employers that optimally reflects their preferences, such that employees are equivalent to self-employed independent contractors in the autonomy they enjoy. I argue that these legacies are anachronistic holdovers that pretend that the hopes of the earlier pro-market ideal had actually been realized, without clearly recognizing how the earlier ideal depended on an economic system of nearly universal self-employment. The deployment of this earlier discourse about market society in our current world masks the actual subjection of most workers to private government, and misrepresents our actual options by taking off the table a large set of concerns and possibilities for dealing with them. My lectures aim to expose this reality, put the constitution of workplace government back on the table as a subject for political discussion, and challenge the dominant constitution of workplace government, which assigns arbitrary and unaccountable power to employers.

I don't wish to attempt to realize the failed ideal of earlier pro-market thinkers. I embrace the prosperity that can only be achieved through large-scale workplaces, and accept that the only feasible way to govern such complex workplaces involves a hierarchy of offices, and hence of authority. So I don't object to government—authority—in the workplace. Cowen argues that owners or managers have certain kinds of expertise in working with the firm's capital that justifies their having authority. To the extent that this is true, it justifies their holding *limited* authority within the firm. I object, not to limited government, but to *private* government—the subjection of workers to arbitrary, unaccountable government, in which they have no voice other than what their employers care to give them (which is often none at all) and are vulnerable to abuses of power. A free society of equals cannot be founded on an institutional structure in which the vast majority of workers for most of their productive lives labor under such government.

The point of my lectures is to clear the ideological ground so that we can put issues of workplace governance on the political agenda, and to provide a framework—the idea of private government—within which to articulate what is problematic about the dominant constitution of workplace governance. I do not propose to solve the question of what the best workplace constitution ought to be. I discuss four ways to promote the freedom and equality of workers: exit, rule of law constraints on employers, constitutional rights, and voice. I argue that the first three alone are not sufficient—workers need *some* voice within the workplace to protect against employer abuses of power, and, more generally, to empower them to assert their standing, respectability, and autonomy interests in the workplace. But

I leave open for further investigation and experimentation the ways that voice is best institutionalized. I also leave open the question of how to balance the four different means for supporting the freedom and equality of workers. I agree with Cowen that consideration of costs and benefits is relevant to this question.

We disagree on two fundamental questions. First, are the problems I identify with workplace governance so rare that it is not worth considering alterations of its constitution to address them? Cowen doubts whether significant numbers of workers have it so bad under private government. Second, how should we determine the costs and benefits of alternative workplace constitutions? Cowen implicitly accepts individual worker and employer choices *within* the current constitution of workplace governance as the measure of what they want.

Consider first the extent of the problem. I am not surprised that Cowen—a highly esteemed superstar tenured academic with wages, job security, working conditions, autonomy, and esteem near the peak of what is available for nonexecutive employees in the United States—is delighted with how great the wage labor system works for *him*. The people with whom he is likely acquainted, similarly occupying the top few percent of the system, are no doubt similarly pleased. However, it appears that he has little notion of what work is like for those at the bottom of the workplace hierarchy, who mostly labor out of public view. As an economist, he also has a professional bias against taking qualitative information, such as workers' narratives and articulated complaints, seriously. He could start by reading Barbara Ehrenreich's reporting on what it is like to work as a low-wage worker in a restaurant, elder care facility, and in retail.[17] Half of all U.S. workers make less than $29,000 annually.[18] I'm guessing that's about one-tenth of Cowen's income.

Has he bothered to check what working conditions are like for workers in the bottom half, who toil in agriculture, slaughterhouses, janitorial services, restaurant work, warehouses, call centers, retail sales, domestic service, elder care, the garment industry, prisons, yard work, and unskilled construction and manufacturing work?

Aggregate statistics are hard to come by, because complaints about employer abuse and oppressive working conditions are so diverse, and cross-industry surveys on qualitative issues are expensive and rare. Moreover, academic research on labor is marginalized and underfunded, as workers themselves are. Here are some indications. Among restaurant workers, 90 percent report being subject to sexual harassment.[19] Between 2007 and 2012, the Department of Labor conducted more than 1,500 investigations of garment factories in Southern California, discovering labor violations, including "sweatshoplike conditions," 93 percent of the time.[20] A recent study of workers in the poultry industry found that the "vast majority" were not allowed adequate bathroom breaks. Many are forced to wear diapers. Employers threaten to fire workers who complain, indicating that their free speech as well as their basic physiological needs and dignity are infringed by their employer.[21] This is just one part of a long and *continuing* struggle by workers in the United States to gain the right to use the bathroom at work—a right workers in other rich countries have long taken for granted.[22]

A recent study, based on a survey of managers and employees, estimates that about seven million workers have been pressured by their bosses to favor some political candidate or issue, by threats of job loss, wage cuts, or plant closure.[23] OSHA relies on employers to report the millions of cases of worker injuries and thousands of deaths suffered by workers each year. Although these harms cannot all be attributed to workplace authoritarianism, underreporting can: a Government Accounting Office study found that 67 percent of occupational health practitioners observed "worker fear of disciplinary action for reporting an injury or illness."[24] Both workers' safety and their freedom of speech are thereby compromised by dictatorship at work. The same report also finds that more than one-third of occupational health practitioners were pressured by employers to underdiagnose and undertreat worker injuries so as to avoid reporting requirements (as minor injuries do not have to be reported to OSHA).[25]

Employers unilaterally determine work schedules, with no employee input for half of all early career employees. The results—including unpredictable schedules (41 percent of workers), fluctuating and short-notice on-call and split-shift work (where employees are sent home and called back the same day)—wreak havoc with the private lives of workers: they can't arrange child care, can't clear their schedules to take college classes or take on a second job needed to cover necessary expenses, and are left with unpaid junk time on their hands in the middle of the day, often hours from home, and with no opportunity to spend it with friends and family.[26]

Walmart, which employs nearly 1 percent of the U.S. labor force (1.4 million workers), is notorious for assigning unreliable schedules to workers. Yet, it is telling that OURWalmart, a nonunion workers' organization dedicated to improving working conditions at Walmart, stands for Organization United for Respect: members are concerned not simply with wages and hours, but with being treated respectfully. A leading complaint of Walmart workers is rude and abusive managers, who scream at and harass them to get them to work harder. This abusiveness may be due to the fact that lower-level managers themselves are assigned work goals without any consideration of what it takes to meet them, and are constantly harassed by upper management for not working hard enough.[27]

This doesn't even describe the very bottom of America's wage labor system. That is occupied by immigrants, both with visas for low-wage work and undocumented. Often the former are forced by their employers to stay past their visa expiration, because those same employers have confiscated their passports and threatened them with arrest or worse. One U.S. State Department investigation found that "30 percent of migrant laborers surveyed in one California community were victims of labor trafficking and 55 percent were victims of labor abuse."[28] Given that there are many million migrant and/or undocumented workers in the United States, it is reasonable to suppose that the number of victims range from the hundreds of thousands to a few million. Abuses include fraud, being forced to work without pay, rape and sexual harassment, beatings, torture, confinement to the workplace and to squalid housing for which extortionate rent is charged, exhausting hours, isolation, religious compulsion, and psychological manipulation and intimidation.[29] Affected industries include "hotel services, hospitality, sales crews, agriculture, manufacturing, janitorial services, construction, health and elder care, and domestic service."[30] Oh, and also restaurants.[31] This list of industries, which collectively employ tens of millions of workers, is telling. Cutting across diverse sectors of the economy, it indicates not only where vulnerable immigrants, but where U.S. citizens working in the same places, are liable to suffer serious assaults in their autonomy, standing, and esteem.

I could go on. Volumes could be filled with cases of worker abuse in the United States today. When many millions of workers suffer harassment, abuse, disrespect, and severe constraints on their autonomy, even when off-duty, and when it is plain that neither state laws nor market orderings are sufficient to deal with these problems, isn't it time to seriously consider how empowering workers with voice can improve the situation?

Cowen won't hear of it. He thinks the costs of sweeping, unaccountable employer authority outweigh the benefits. Let's set aside his fallacious arguments—that unemployment is even worse, that employers sometimes censor workers' off-duty speech for good reasons. That some conditions are even worse than living under dictatorship, and that dictators sometimes make decisions that most people like, hardly justifies this form of government. Fundamentally, our disagreement comes down to how to evaluate private government at work. This depends on a disagreement over what institutions are best to judge these matters. Cowen believes that the market decides best. I believe that existing market orderings are distorted by the state's prior allocation of unaccountable power to employers over employees. Market outcomes thereby grossly undervalue the costs to workers of private government. Let's see how this works in relation to Cowen's four arguments that the market is the best judge of the values at stake: employer competition for workers, compensating differentials, worker exit, and efficiency.

Cowen argues that employers have to compete for talent, and this makes them respect workers' autonomy and dignity. "The desire to attract and keep talent is the single biggest reason why companies try to create pleasant and tolerant atmospheres for their workers." I agree with his statement: *when* workers are respected by their employers, this is the main reason why. It doesn't follow that all workers *do* get respected by their employers. Rather, *the amount of respect, standing, and autonomy they get is roughly proportional to their market value.* Employers don't have to compete for workers who aren't scarce: those

who are unskilled, inexperienced, living in areas with high unemployment, or with other liabilities, such as an arrest record
or a disability. That's a lot of workers. Blacks, for example, who
are about 12 percent of the labor force, suffer from virtually
permanent double-digit unemployment rates. Workers of all
races who live in towns devastated from plant closures due to
competition from abroad also suffer from high unemployment,
because their mobility is low.[32] Much of the time, the entire
economy operates in periods of substantial unemployment or
underemployment, affecting workers generally: even if they
have a job, the cost of job loss is so high they have to put up
with nearly any abuse just to hang on to an income. Meanwhile,
employers use their power to design workplaces to create a
fine-grained division of labor in which workers are deskilled
and thus easily replaceable.

Cowen argues that workers get compensated with higher
wages when employers impose adverse working conditions on
them, and that, if anything, the tax code biases the market in
favor of too many "perks" and not enough wages. I don't think we
should trivialize basic requirements of human dignity and well-
being, such as freedom to use the bathroom, as mere "perks."
Cowen also ignores how the state has countered its purported
tax bias by placing a very heavy thumb on the scales against
worker autonomy, standing, and dignity, through its legal establishment of dictatorship as the default constitution of workplace
governance. Still, Cowen is correct that *some* high-wage workers
enjoy *some* compensation for bad conditions, such as grueling
hours. I have explained elsewhere that even when they do, this
does not account for all their concerns. They still retain an interest in having a say over their working conditions.[33]

Here I stress a different point: I doubt whether Cowen's
model applies across the entire spectrum of wage labor. For the

most part, lower-paid workers suffer from higher levels of disrespect, harassment, terrible working conditions, and offensive restraints on autonomy than higher-paid workers. Moreover, heightening the profit motive makes things worse all-around for these workers. For example, when prisons are converted from public to private, for-profit enterprises, guards simultaneously suffer huge wage cuts *and* large increases in violent assaults by prisoners, because their employers also cut staffing levels so low that not enough guards are available to control the prisoners.[34] Inmate attacks on staff in federal prisons increase by 260 percent.[35]

Cowen's confidence that workers are somehow compensated with higher wages for putting up with gross insults to their dignity, standing, and autonomy is belied by the staggering scale of wage theft in America. Wage theft is pervasive among low-wage construction, restaurant, garment, nursing home, agriculture, and poultry workers, and affects many middle-class workers as well.[36] One estimate from a *business-funded* think tank indicated an annual wage theft tab at $19 billion in 2004—likely a gross underestimate, given its source.[37] Another estimate puts the tab at $50 billion in 2014, affecting two-thirds of workers in low-wage industries, costing them nearly 15 percent of their total earnings. This is more than three times the amount of all other thefts in the United States.[38] If employers have so little regard for their employees that they steal their wages, how likely is it that they are making it up to them by according them better working conditions? The more plausible model, supported by observation of what work is like for the bottom half (at least), is that employers' contempt for workers' basic dignity, standing, and autonomy is simultaneously expressed in the low wages they pay and the appalling conditions they force their employees to endure. The scale of wage theft also supports the claim that private government has an inherent tendency to overstep its legal bounds. In the absence of internal checks by which workers can hold their employers accountable, employers will not merely exercise the authority they have by law, but abuse their power.

To the extent that Cowen is willing to concede these problems, his sole suggested remedy is to enhance workers' powers of exit. I am glad to see him, if only by implication, climb on board the campaign to abolish noncompete clauses, which forbid workers from taking their human capital with them when they quit. And I wholeheartedly agree with him on the urgency of guaranteeing exit rights to immigrants on work visas. Nevertheless, the suggestion that enhancing exit rights alone would be sufficient to deal with the problems I have documented is not credible. What jobs are workers supposed to exit *to*? When 90 percent of waitresses experience sexual harassment, they have no reliable place to escape it, other than by leaving their industry-specific skills behind—and even then, not so much, since sexual harassment exists in all industries. Add to this the problems of unemployment, underemployment, ineligibility for unemployment insurance for "voluntary" quits, and it's easy to see how unhelpful "why don't you just leave?" is as advice to workers. When workers have only exit rights and no voice, this amounts to a grant to the dictatorial employer to harvest the *entire* "producer's surplus"—all the benefits that make their job better than workers' next best alternative—that would otherwise accrue to workers before the job gets so intolerable that they quit. Indeed, given the uncertainties about whether conditions would be better elsewhere (extremely difficult for non-employees to determine), and the steep costs of job loss under any realistic scenario, an exit-rights-only regime in effect grants to dictatorial employers the power to appropriate considerably more than the workers' producer surplus before they leave.

Cowen's final appeal is to "efficiency." He worries that we can't have nice things if workers don't submit to the dictatorial power of their employers. This is the same argument British West Indies sugar growers made in Parliament in defense of slavery, during the debates over abolition.[39] Even considered in its own terms, the argument is highly dubious. Cowen cites a single study suggesting that the German system of codetermination depresses profits. Supposing that profits are lower under the German system, the wonder is why this isn't seen as a point in favor of the Germans, in that the people who actually do the work enjoy greater shares of the pie. Cowen thinks it is a point against, because it depresses productivity. The evidence is mixed. Some studies find that codetermination has positive or neutral effects on productivity, at least in larger firms.[40] I suggest that if productivity effects are that hard to consistently detect, they are probably not significant.

Cowen notes that "when workers have a say in governance, employment tends to be more stable and wages tend to be more volatile." This is a striking concession, given that the U.S. economy has had a chronic tendency to unemployment or underemployment. There is no greater waste, from an efficiency point of view, than unemployment. Moreover, the neat efficiency claims about market allocations in any given market apply only in the context of full employment. Finally, it is worth noting that the powers employers routinely exercise vastly exceed any authority that could be justified on efficiency or any other grounds. None of the sexual harassment suffered by workers improves productivity. It's a sheer abuse of power, and a massive dead-weight loss of utility, even if we view matters solely in terms of efficiency.

We should reject Cowen's terms in any event. Economic concepts of efficiency accept current endowments of property rights as the normative baseline against which to measure improvements. Precisely what is contested here are the baseline governance rights attached to capital ownership. Cowen thus begs the question in favor of workplace dictatorship by choosing efficiency as his measure. Moreover, the decision to adopt efficiency as measured by market outcomes is a decision to value workers' interests in inverse proportion to their marginal utility of wealth.[41] By that perverse measure, the most trifling interests of the wealthy can outweigh the most vital and fundamental interests of the poor.

I advocate a different way to determine the value of workers' dignity and autonomy: let workers speak for themselves in the context of a system of workplace governance in which they have a voice. The successful implementation of voice in European systems of codetermination already demonstrates that empowering workers in this way is both feasible and compatible with an extraordinarily high level of prosperity. My point is not to endorse the German model of codetermination. There is plenty of room to experiment with alternative constitutions that guarantee workers' voices, and to consider the costs and benefits of these alternatives. My point is also not to impose any particular combination of what Cowen calls "perks" over wages. Within a workplace government that guarantees workers a voice, managers will be free to offer different packages of wages and working conditions, and workers will be free to suggest alternative packages, negotiate, and vote on trade-offs. My point is simply that workers need some kind of institutionalized voice at work to ensure that their interests are heard, that they are respected, and that they have some share of autonomy in workplace decisions. Subjecting them to private government—to arbitrary, unaccountable authority—is no way to treat people who have a claim to dignity, autonomy, and standing no less than that of their employers.

Notes

Author's Preface

1. Barbara Ehrenreich, *Nickel and Dimed: On (not) Getting by in America* (New York: Holt Paperbacks, 2008), 157.
2. *Frlekin v. Apple, Inc.*, 2015 U.S. Dist. LEXIS 151937 (N.D. Cal., Nov. 7, 2015) (dismissing on summary judgment employees' claim that Apple violated minimum wage law in failing to pay them for time spent waiting to be inspected, notwithstanding the law's definition of "hours worked" as "the time during which an employee is subject to the control of an employer," because during that time, employees are not allowed to work).
3. Oxfam America, *No Relief: Denial of Bathroom Breaks in the Poultry Industry* (Washington, D.C., 2016), 2, https://www.oxfamamerica.org/static/media/files/No_Relief_Embargo.pdf.
4. William Becker, Salimah Meghani, Jeanette Tetrault, and David Fiellin, "Racial/Ethnic Differences in Report of Drug

Testing Practices at the Workplace Level in the U.S.," *American Journal on Addictions* 23, no. 4 (2014): 357–62.

5. Alexander Hertel-Fernandez and Paul Secunda, "Citizens Coerced: A Legislative Fix for Workplace Political Intimidation Post–Citizens United," *UCLA Law Review* 64 (2016): 1, http://ssrn.com/abstract=2740649.

Chapter 1

1. Of course, this usage of the term "left" is anachronistic. But it serves to fix ideas. I hasten to add that some egalitarians of the seventeenth and eighteenth centuries—notably, the Diggers and Rousseau—rejected market society. My focus in this lecture is on those who embraced it.

2. Adam Smith, *An Inquiry into the Nature and Causes of the Wealth of Nations, vol. 1,* Glasgow Edition of the Works and Correspondence of Adam Smith (Indianapolis: Liberty Fund, 1981), I.ii.2.

3. Karl Marx, *Capital: A Critique of Political Economy*, edited by Frederick Engels, translated by Samuel Moore and Edward Aveling (Chicago: Charles H. Kerr, 1912), 195–96.

4. This is not just cynicism on Smith's part. He points to a transcultural social fact, that every gift implies a debt that, until reciprocated in kind, subordinates the recipient to the giver. See Marcel Mauss, *The Gift*, translated by I. Cunnison (New York: Norton, 1967); William Miller, *Humiliation* (Ithaca, NY: Cornell University Press, 1993), ch. 1.

5. Marx, *Capital*, 195.

6. Thus, the so-called Adam Smith problem—the purported tension between Smith's moral theory, founded on sympathy with others, and his economics, supposedly founded on pure egoism, is dissolved.

7. "All for ourselves, and nothing for other people, seems, in every age of the world, to have been the vile maxim of the masters of mankind." Smith, *Wealth of Nations, vol. 1,* III.iv.10.

8. On this point, I fully agree with Pierre Rosanvallon, *The Society of Equals,* translated by Arthur Goldhammer (Cambridge, MA: Harvard University Press, 2013), 11, 29, 51.

9. For the first statement of the army's program, see "Agreement of the People," in *The English Levellers,* edited by Andrew Sharp (New York: Cambridge University Press, 1998), 92–101. "Agitators"—Leveller officers chosen by their men—debated this proposal with Cromwell and Ireton at Putney in 1647. The Putney debates offer some of the most riveting reading in the history of political thought, at a level of intellectual depth and seriousness vastly exceeding contemporary public discourse. See "Putney Debates," in *Puritanism and Liberty, Being the Army Debates (1647–9) from the Clarke Manuscripts with Supplementary Documents,* ed. A.S.P. Woodhouse (Chicago: University of Chicago Press, 1951), 1–124.

10. "Putney Debates, 29 October 1647," *Puritanism and Liberty,* 75.

11. John Lilburne, William Walwyn, Thomas Prince, and Richard Overton, "An Agreement of the Free People of England, 1 May 1649," in *The Levellers: Miscellaneous Writings,* ed. James Otteson, vol. 4 of *The Levellers: Overton, Walwyn and Lilburne* (Bristol, UK: Thoemmes Press, 2003), articles XXX, XVIII, XX, XIX.

12. John Lilburne, "Englands Birth-Right Justified," in *Works of John Lilburne,* edited by Otteson, vol. 3 of *The Levellers,* 62–64.

13. John Lilburne, "Londons Liberty in Chains Discovered," in *Works of John Lilburne,* 175–77.

14. William Walwyn, "For a Free Trade," in *Works of William Walwyn*, vol. 2 of *The Levellers*, edited by Otteson, 399–405.
15. It would be anachronistic to attribute such ideas to any seventeenth-century thinkers because the modern notion of distributive justice was not invented until the end of the eighteenth century. Samuel Fleischacker, *A Short History of Distributive Justice* (Cambridge, MA: Harvard University Press, 2004).
16. See "The Root and Branch Petition (1640)," *Documents Illustrative of English Church History*, edited by Henry Gee and William John Hardy (New York: Macmillan, 1896), 537–45, http://history.hanover.edu/texts/engref/er97.html, a contemporary document calling for an end to the church's powers in these respects.
17. Thomas Leng, "'His Neighbours Land Mark': William Sykes and the Campaign for 'Free Trade' in Civil War England," *Historical Research* 86, no. 232 (2013): 230–52.
18. William Blackstone, *Commentaries on the Laws of England*, 1st ed. (Oxford: Clarendon Press, 1765), ch. 15.
19. For some legal complexities in the early modern era, see Karen Pearlston, "Review of *Women, Property, and the Letters of the Law in Early Modern England*," *Osgoode Hall Law Journal* 44, no. 1 (2006): 219–21; for documentation of women's contestation of husbands' authority, along with contemporary cultural recognition of its limits, see Don Herzog, *Household Politics: Conflict in Early Modern England* (New Haven, CT: Yale University Press, 2013).
20. Recall John Locke, *Second Treatise of Government* (Indianapolis: Hackett, 1980), §77: "The first society was between man and wife, which gave beginning to that between parents and children; to which, in time, that between master and servant came to be added . . . and make up but one

family, wherein the master or mistress of it had some sort of rule proper to a family." Locke here includes employees in the family, and represents it as a kind of government, which, in the state of nature, is not essentially patriarchal. I shall return to Locke's feminism later in this lecture.

21. See Blackstone, *Commentaries*, ch. 14; Karen Orren, *Belated Feudalism: Labor, the Law, and Liberal Development in the United States* (Cambridge: Cambridge University Press, 1991) (documenting the early modern English law of master and servant, and how it continued to govern U.S. employment relations well into the nineteenth century).

22. See Don Herzog, *Happy Slaves* (Chicago: University of Chicago Press, 1989), ch. 1.

23. Arthur O. Lovejoy, *The Great Chain of Being: A Study of the History of an Idea* (Cambridge, MA: Harvard University Press, 1936).

24. Robert Filmer, *Patriarcha: Or the Natural Power of Kings* (London: W. Davis, 1680).

25. Christopher Hill, *The World Turned Upside Down: Radical Ideas during the English Revolution* (New York: Penguin Books, 1991), 155.

26. See Saint Augustine, *City of God*, translated by Marcus Dods (Edinburgh: T. & T. Clark, 1888), XIX.15.

27. Hill, *World Turned Upside Down*, chs. 3, 4.

28. Herzog, *Happy Slaves*, ch. 1.

29. See Hill, *World Turned Upside Down*, esp. ch. 8; Andrew Bradstock, *Radical Religion in Cromwell's England: A Concise History from the English Civil War to the End of the Commonwealth* (New York: I. B. Tauris, 2011), esp. ch. 5. Thus arose the endlessly repeated conservative charge that egalitarians believe in the perfectibility of human beings. Absurd as applied to today's believers in an egalitarian distribution of

income and wealth, democracy, and other secular egalitarian doctrines, the charge makes sense as applied to historical Christian millennialist egalitarian social movements, which needed to refute the authoritarian doctrine of original sin.

30. Samuel Torshell, *The Womans Glorie: A Treatise, First, Asserting the Due Honour of That Sexe, by Manifesting That Women Are Capable of the Highest Improvements and Instancing Severall Examples of Womens Eminencies . . . ,* 2nd ed. (London: Printed for John Bellamy, 1650), 11.

31. Hill, *World Turned Upside Down*, 310–12.

32. John Lilburne, "The Free-Man's Freedom Vindicated," *Works of John Lilburne*, 105–6.

33. Elizabeth Chidley, "Petition of Women, Affecters and Approvers of the Petition of Sept. 11, 1648 (5th May 1649)," in *Puritanism and Liberty*, 367.

34. Hill, *World Turned Upside Down*, 312.

35. "Root and Branch Petition," articles 10, 12, 24.

36. Michael Levy, "Freedom, Property and the Levellers: The Case of John Lilburne," *Western Political Quarterly* 36, no. 1 (1983): 116–133, here 120.

37. See Walwyn, "For a Free Trade," 403–4 (complaining that the burdens of guild government lie "more heavily upon the more moderate Traders" who suffer from the guilds' "many unreasonable Orde Oathes, fines, Censures" and that they spend too much time "in Courts & meetings about others affaires").

38. Leng, "'His Neighbours Land Mark,'" 233, 236.

39. Thomas Johnson, *A Plea for Free-Mens Liberties: Or the Monopoly of the Eastland Merchants* (London, 1646), 2, 3, http://gateway.proquest.com/openurl?ctx_ver=Z39.88 -2003&res_id=xri:eebo&rft_id=xri:eebo:citation:9986 1268.

40. Walwyn, "For a Free Trade," 403.

41. Ibid., 402, 401.

42. Johnson, *Plea*, 4.

43. "Reason being the fountain of all honest laws, gives to every man propriety and liberty; propriety of interest, freedom of enjoyment and improovement to his own advantage . . . those who have bereft us of our liberty, have made bold with our propriety" (ibid.).

44. Jacqueline Stevens, "The Reasonableness of Locke's Majority: Property Rights, Consent, and Resistance in the Second Treatise," *Political Theory* 24, no. 3 (1996): 423–63.

45. As Jeremy Waldron decisively demonstrates, in *God, Locke, and Equality: Christian Foundations of John Locke's Political Thought* (Cambridge: Cambridge University Press, 2002), ch. 2.

46. "As justice gives every man a title to the product of his honest industry . . . so charity gives every man a title to so much out of another's plenty, as will keep him from extreme want, where he has no means to subsist otherwise: and a man can no more justly make use of another's necessity to force him to become his vassal, by with-holding that relief God requires him to afford to the wants of his brother, than he that has more strength can seize upon a weaker, master him to his obedience, and with a dagger at his throat, offer his death or slavery." John Locke, "First Treatise of Government," *The Works of John Locke in Nine Volumes*, 12th ed. (London: Rivington, 1824), §42.

47. Smith, *Wealth of Nations*, vol. 1, III.4.4 (emphasis added).

48. Ibid., III.4.5–8.

49. Ibid., III.4.9.

50. Ibid., III.4.10.

51. Ibid., III.4.11–15.

52. Ibid., III.2.6.

53. Ibid., III.2.7.

54. Ibid., III.2.8–13.
55. Ibid., III.4.19.
56. Smith, *Wealth of Nations*, vol. 2, V.1.E.32. Joint-stock corporations tend to fail because their governance structure cannot solve the principal–agent problem of holding directors accountable to investors. Surveying the history of joint-stock corporations, Smith finds that directors lack expertise, initiative, and energy because they are risking other people's money, and allow employees to squander the corporation's resources (ibid., V.1.E.18, 27).
57. Smith, *Wealth of Nations*, vol. 1, I.ix.20. It follows that, while a free market economy would be more unequal than primitive society, it would be far more equal than a feudal or mercantilist economy. For further support of the view that Smith's vision of a free market society has egalitarian tendencies, see Deborah Boucoyannis, "The Equalizing Hand: Why Adam Smith Thought the Market Should Produce Wealth without Steep Inequality," *Perspectives on Politics* 11, no. 4 (2013): 1051–70.
58. Smith, *Wealth of Nations*, vol. 1, I.1.3.
59. Other Enlightenment figures shared this view: "It is easy to prove that fortunes tend naturally toward equality, and that excessive differences of wealth either cannot exist or must promptly cease, if the civil laws do not establish artificial ways of perpetuating and amassing such fortunes, and if freedom of commerce and industry eliminate the advantage that any prohibitive law or fiscal privilege gives to acquired wealth." Antoine-Nicholas Condorcet, *Outlines of an Historical View of the Progress of the Human Mind* (Chicago: G. Langer, 2009), 10th epoch.
60. Medicine was so unreliable that one might be better off not being able to afford a doctor's services. No one could

travel in comfort or speed at any expense. The penny press made news available to all. Theaters offered cheap seats. No wonder Smith disparaged the quest for great wealth as not worth the trouble. See *The Theory of Moral Sentiments*, edited by D. D. Raphael and A. L. Macfie, Glasgow Edition of the Works and Correspondence of Adam Smith (Oxford: Oxford University Press, 1976), I.3.2.1, III.3.31, IV.1.6.8.

61. Smith, *Wealth of Nations*, vol. 1, III.4.16.

62. So was the fact that the hope was predicated on mass, violent expropriation of land from its former possessors. In contrast to slavery, which received substantial attention from many Euro-American egalitarians, Native American claims received little attention.

63. Joyce Appleby, *Capitalism and a New Social Order: The Republican Vision of the 1790s*, (New York: New York University Press, 1984), 89; Eric Foner, *Tom Paine and Revolutionary America* (New York: Oxford University Press, 1976), 32, 43–44.

64. Thomas Paine, *Rights of Man. Part the Second: Combining Principle and Practice*, 8th ed. (London: J. S. Jordan, 1792), 7–8.

65. Ibid., 59n*.

66. Ibid., 60.

67. See for example, Paine, *Rights of Man, Part 2*, 82; Thomas Paine, *The Crisis: In Thirteen Numbers. Written during the Late War. By the Author of Common Sense* (Albany, NY: Charles and George Webster, 1792), no. 3, 40.

68. Paine, *Rights of Man, Part 2*, 150.

69. Foner, *Paine and Revolutionary America*, 183–200.

70. See ibid., ch. 5, for an extended discussion of Paine's thought and activities regarding price controls.

71. Ibid., 190.

72. Paine, *Rights of Man, Part 2*, 16.
73. Ibid., 69.
74. Ibid., 3–4.
75. Ibid., 113–31.
76. The Republican Party, however, has not followed Paine in other respects: his critique of Christianity (Thomas Paine, *The Age of Reason* [Boston: Thomas Hall, 1794]); his feminism (see Eileen Hunt Botting, "Thomas Paine amidst the Early Feminists," in *Selected Writings of Thomas Paine*, edited by Ian Shapiro and Jane Calvert [New Haven, CT: Yale University Press, 2014], 630–54); his opposition to the death penalty; his opposition to military spending, war, and imperialism. Most of all, Paine, who experienced poverty for much of his life, had profound sympathy for the poor and never disparaged them as lazy, lacking enterprise, or corrupted by "welfare." As we shall see, he argued that everyone had a right to sufficient income to avoid poverty.
77. Craig Calhoun, *The Roots of Radicalism: Tradition, the Public Sphere, and Early Nineteenth-Century Social Movements* (Chicago: University of Chicago Press, 2012).
78. Paine, *Rights of Man, Part 2*, 11.
79. Ibid., 63, 100.
80. Ibid., 92–98.
81. Ibid., 67–69.
82. Ibid., 105–6. When Paine complained that people on government pay were parasites, he was not speaking of magistrates, parish officials, or other government workers who perform actual public services for modest pay. He was complaining of the court, and of sinecures. Genuine civil servants, by contrast, are entitled to reasonable pay (ibid., 54, 72, 119).

83. Ibid., 4, 77–80, 87, 100–102, 155. In contrast to the U.S. Republican Party today, Paine opposed regressive consumption taxes and supported taxes on inheritances and bonds.

84. Thomas Paine, *Common Sense* (Edinburgh: Eighteenth Century Collections Online; Gale, 1776), 33.

85. Paine expressed his objection to wage controls, and preference for market wages, in an era when regulations set *maximum* wages.

86. Thomas Paine, "Agrarian Justice," *The Writings of Thomas Paine, Vol. III (1791–1804)*, edited by Moncure Daniel Conway (New York: Putnam's Sons, 1894), 322–44.

87. Eric Foner, *Free Soil, Free Labor, Free Men: The Ideology of the Republican Party before the Civil War*, with a new introduction (New York: Oxford University Press, 1995), is the indispensable work on this subject.

88. James Henry Hammond, "Speech in the Senate, 35th Congress, Session 1," *Congressional Globe*, March 4, 1858: 71.

89. Abraham Lincoln, "Annual Address before the Wisconsin State Agricultural Society, at Milwaukee, September 30, 1859," *Abraham Lincoln, Complete Works*, edited by John Nicolay and John Hay, vol. 1 (New York: Century Co., 1859), 581.

90. "There is no permanent class of hired laborers amongst us. . . . The hired laborer of yesterday, labors on his own account to-day; and will hire others to labor for him to-morrow. Advancement—improvement in condition—is the order of things in a society of equals." Abraham Lincoln, "Fragment on Free Labor," *Collected Works of Abraham Lincoln, Vol. 3*, edited by Roy Basler (New Brunswick, NJ: Rutgers University Press, 1859), 463.

91. Foner, *Free Soil*, Kindle loc. 332–37.

92. Ibid., Kindle loc. 434.

93. Ibid., Kindle loc. 377–80.

94. Lincoln, "Address before the Wisconsin State Agricultural Society," 581–82.

95. Lincoln may have baked it into the ideological infrastructure of his party. A century and a half after his pronouncement, Eric Cantor, then Republican House majority leader, tweeted on Labor Day 2012: "Today, we celebrate those who have taken a risk, worked hard, built a business and earned their own success," https://twitter.com/ericcantor/status/242654833218293760. Cantor appears to be viscerally incapable of recognizing how a day could be dedicated to honoring wage laborers.

96. Sean Wilentz, *Chants Democratic: New York City and the Rise of the American Working Class, 1788–1850* (New York: Oxford University Press, 2004), 508–16.

97. Gertrude Himmelfarb, *The Idea of Poverty: England in the Early Industrial Age* (New York: Knopf, 1984), 78. See, for example, Jeremy Bentham, *Pauper Management Improved: Particularly by Means of an Application of the Panopticon Principle of Construction* (London: R. Baldwin, 1812).

98. Isaac Kramnick, *Republicanism and Bourgeois Radicalism: Political Ideology in Late Eighteenth-Century England and America* (Ithaca, NY: Cornell University Press, 1990), 97.

99. Smith, *Wealth of Nations*, vol. 2, V.1.F.50.

100. Smith, *Theory of Moral Sentiments*, I.3.3.1.

Chapter 2

1. This is true of the corporate form. Legally, the corporation, *not* the shareholders, owns the firm's assets. In a partnership, an oligarchy governs and owns all the assets.

2. R. H. Coase, "The Nature of the Firm," *Economica* 4, no. 16 (1937): 386–405.

3. Eugene Volokh, "Private Employees' Speech and Political Activity: Statutory Protection against Employer Retaliation" (2012), http://ssrn.com/abstract=2174776.

4. Ken Cuccinelli, *The Last Line of Defense: The New Fight for American Liberty* (New York: Crown Forum, 2013), 52, 231.

5. This may sound like a positivist account of *law*. But government need not rule by law—that is, general rules of conduct. It can rule by orders or decrees, issued ad hoc to particular persons for particular occasions. I take no stand here regarding a positivist account of law.

6. Max Weber, *Economy and Society*, edited by Guenther Roth and Claus Wittich (Berkeley: University of California Press, 1968), 56.

7. John Adams, "Letter to Abigail, April 14, 1776," *Letters of John Adams Addressed to His Wife*, edited by Charles Adams, vol. 1 (Boston: C. C. Little and J. Brown, 1841), 96–97.

8. I draw on Herzog, *Household Politics*, 89–94, who spends more time distinguishing the entailments of privacy than I do here.

9. Here I focus on "external" conceptions of positive freedom in terms of opportunity sets within individuals' budget constraints, legal permissions, and other external conditions. I set aside psychological notions of positive freedom, such as freedom from addictions, compulsions, or other motives with which the agent does not identify.

10. Philip Pettit, *Republicanism: A Theory of Freedom and Government* (New York: Oxford University Press, 1997), 5.

11. See, for example, Milton Friedman, *Capitalism and Freedom* (Chicago: University of Chicago Press, 1962), linking private property to political and not just economic freedom.

12. Joyce Shaw Peterson, *American Automobile Workers, 1900–1933* (Albany: State University of New York Press, 1987), 57, 72.

13. Natasha Singer, "Health Plan Penalty Ends at Penn State," *New York Times,* September 19, 2013, http://www.nytimes .com/2013/09/19/business/after-uproar-penn-state-suspends -penalty-fee-in-wellness-plan.html.

14. Coase, "Nature of the Firm."

15. Oliver Williamson, "Markets and Hierarchies: Some Elementary Considerations," *American Economic Review* 63, no. 2 (1973): 316–25, here 322.

16. Coase, "Nature of the Firm," 388.

17. Ibid., 391.

18. Only fifteen states do not allow a disclaimer to count as a per se defense against a charge of wrongful discharge under an implied-contract exception to employment-at-will; twenty-two states allow disclaimers and limit implied-contract exceptions to written documents; thirteen states do not recognize any implied-contract exception to employment-at-will. Charles Muhl, "The Employment-at-Will Doctrine: Three Major Exceptions," *Monthly Labor Review,* January 2001: 5.

19. *Nelson v. Knight,* Iowa Supreme Court, No. 11-1857, July 12, 2013.

20. Neela Banerjee, "Ohio Miners Say They Were Forced to Attend Romney Rally," *Los Angeles Times,* August 29, 2012, http://articles.latimes.com/2012/aug/29/news/la -pn-miners-romney-rally-20120829/.

21. Dugan Arnett, "Nightmare in Maryville: Teens' Sexual Encounter Ignites a Firestorm against Family," *Kansas City Star,* October 12, 2013, http://www.kansascity.com /news/special-reports/maryville/article329412/Nightmare

-in-Maryville-Teens%E2%80%99-sexual-encounter-ignites
-a-firestorm-against-family.html.

22. Armen Alchian and Harold Demsetz, "Production, Information Costs, and Economic Organization," *American Economic Review* 62, no. 5 (1972): 777–95, here 777.

23. Even the addition of immigration rights to new governments—something workers do not enjoy at work—does not dissolve their authority. Within the European Union (EU), citizens are guaranteed the right not only to exit but also to enter other member states. Yet this has not eliminated the authority of EU member states.

24. Michael Jensen and William Meckling, "Theory of the Firm: Managerial Behavior, Agency Costs and Ownership Structure," *Journal of Financial Economics* 3 (1976): 305–60, here 310.

25. John Tomasi, *Free Market Fairness* (Princeton, NJ: Princeton University Press, 2012), 23, 77, 81.

26. This tendency facilitates a common abuse of labor law, in which employers pretend that their employees are independent contractors, to avoid minimum wage, maximum hours, benefits and safety regulations; to shift the burden of employment taxes on their workers; and to force them to pay for equipment and uniforms. The court test in such cases is always whether the employer exercises control over the worker. See, for example, *Alexander v. FedEx Ground Package System*, 2014 U.S. App. LEXIS 16585 (9th Cir. Aug. 27, 2014), which ruled that FedEx misclassified thousands of its California truck drivers as independent contractors.

27. Josiah Wedgwood, a pioneer of the Industrial Revolution in promoting worker discipline in his pottery factory, was also a major abolitionist.

28. Blackstone, *Commentaries*, ch. 14.

29. Karen Orren tells the story for the United States in *Belated Feudalism*. Similar developments took place in other common law countries and the rest of Western Europe during the nineteenth century. An important lesson of her work is that some nineteenth-century labor law legal doctrines in the United States and England that are thought to be novelties of laissez-faire free contract ideology—for example, that an employer could confiscate a worker's entire accrued wage for the slightest insubordination—were in fact merely continuations of English labor laws established in the feudal era. In other words, laissez faire at the level of market relations left feudal authoritarianism intact at the level of intrafirm relations.

30. Robert Allen, "Engels' Pause: A Pessimist's Guide to the British Industrial Revolution," *Explorations in Economic History* 46, no. 4 (2009): 418–35.

31. Under employment-at-will, the legal reach of employers' authority extended to the entire day, as it still does today except when expressly limited by law or contract, or, in fifteen states, by implied contract. However, for practical purposes, the separation of the workplace from the home substantially raised the costs and reduced the benefits to many employers of reaching that far, and thereby opened up room for workers to enjoy freedom from their bosses when off duty.

32. As I argue in Elizabeth Anderson, "Equality and Freedom in the Workplace: Recovering Republican Insights," *Social Philosophy and Policy* 31, no. 2 (2015): 48–69. One consequence of this point is that the traditional libertarian argument that the state should simply stop "interfering" with the economy is misguided: it is like saying that the

commissioner of baseball should stop interfering with the game by promulgating its rules. It turns out that to facilitate efficient cooperation at the vast scales of modern developed economies, the rules have to be remarkably complex. This opens up room both for democratic control in the public interest and for regulatory capture.

33. For the classic exposition, see Blackstone, *Commentaries*, ch. 15.

34. As I argue in Anderson, "Equality and Freedom in the Workplace."

35. See, for example, Sidney Pollard, "Factory Discipline in the Industrial Revolution," *Economic History Review* 16, no. 2 (1963): 254–71. He notes the "deliberate or accidental modelling of many [factory] works on workhouses and prisons, a fact well known to the working population" (254). I stress that it did not take Marxists or socialists to see the problem in the terms in which I have presented them. American labor republicans also understood it. See Alex Gourevitch, *From Slavery to the Cooperative Commonwealth: Labor and Republican Liberty in the Nineteenth Century* (New York: Cambridge University Press, 2015).

36. Most famously, the inability of comprehensive centralized planning to use the information needed to allocate resources efficiently. See Friedrich A. Hayek, "The Use of Knowledge in Society," *American Economic Review* 35 (1945): 519–30.

37. Those of you who are adjunct or contingent faculty, on the other hand, understand firsthand what I am talking about.

38. Workplace Democracy Association, "Zogby Poll: As Independence Day Nears, Workplace Democracy Association Survey Finds One in Four Working Americans Describe Their Employer as a 'Dictatorship,'" June 23, 2008, https://

workplacedemocracy.wordpress.com/2008/06/23/work place-democracy-survey/.

39. *Pollock v. Williams*, 322 U.S. 4, at 18 (1944). In this opinion, Justice Jackson, writing for the Supreme Court, struck down a Florida statute criminalizing failure to specifically perform a labor contract on which an advance was made, as contrary to the Thirteenth Amendment prohibition on involuntary servitude. Note the late date of the decision. Risa Goluboff, "The Thirteenth Amendment and a New Deal for Civil Rights," in *The Promises of Liberty: The History and Contemporary Relevance of the Thirteenth Amendment*, edited by Alexander Tsesis (New York: Columbia University Press, 2010), 119–37, explains how Jackson's reasoning reflected New Deal (positive liberty) rather than *Lochner*-era freedom of contract (negative liberty) principles.

40. See Robert Nozick, *Anarchy, State, and Utopia* (New York: Basic Books, 1974), 331; Walter Block, "Toward a Libertarian Theory of Inalienability: A Critique of Rothbard, Barnett, Smith, Kinsella, Gordon, and Epstein," *Journal of Libertarian Studies* 17, no. 2 (2003): 39–85; Stephen Kershnar, "A Liberal Argument for Slavery," *Journal of Social Philosophy* 34, no. 4 (2003): 510–36. For libertarians opposed to the validity of slave contracts, see Murray Rothbard, *The Ethics of Liberty*, rev. ed. (New York: New York University Press, 1998), 40–41; Randy Barnett, "Contract Remedies and Inalienable Rights," *Social Philosophy and Policy* 4, no. 1 (1986): 179–202.

41. Matt Marx, "The Firm Strikes Back: Non-Compete Agreements and the Mobility of Technical Professionals," *American Sociological Review* 76, no. 5 (2011): 695–712; Steven Greenhouse, "Noncompete Clauses Increasingly Pop Up in Array of Jobs," *New York Times*, June 8, 2014,

http://www.nytimes.com/2014/06/09/business/non compete-clauses-increasingly-pop-up-in-array-of-jobs .html; Clare O'Connor, "Does Jimmy John's Non-Compete Clause for Sandwich Makers Have Legal Legs?" *Forbes*, October 15, 2014, http://www.forbes.com/sites/clare oconnor/2014/10/15/does-jimmy-johns-non-compete -clause-for-sandwich-makers-have-legal-legs/.

42. Orly Lobel, *Talent Wants to Be Free: Why We Should Learn to Love Leaks, Raids, and Free Riding* (New Haven, CT: Yale University Press, 2013).

43. Patricia Bromley and John Meyer, "'They Are All Organizations': The Cultural Roots of Blurring between the Nonprofit, Business, and Government Sectors," *Administration & Society* (2014), http://dx.doi.org/10.1177/0095399714548268.

44. There may be legitimate limits to this for higher-ranked managers and press agents who are regarded as official spokespersons for their firms. It is one thing to fire an ordinary Pepsi worker for drinking Coke on the job (Suzanne Presto, "Coke Employee Fired for Drinking Pepsi on the Job," *CNN Money*, June 16 2003, http://money.cnn .com/2003/06/13/news/funny/coke_pepsi/index.htm), and quite another for the CEO of Pepsi to publicly disparage Pepsi in comparison to Coke.

45. Mark Linder and Ingrid Nygaard, *Void Where Prohibited: Rest Breaks and the Right to Urinate on Company Time* (Ithaca, NY: ILR Press, 1998), 46.

46. James Whitman and Gabrielle Friedman, "The European Transformation of Harassment Law," *Columbia Journal of European Law* 9 (2002–3): 241–74.

47. Cynthia Estlund, "Why Workers Still Need a Collective Voice in the Era of Norms and Mandates," *Research Handbook on the Economics of Labor and Employment Law*, edited

by Cynthia Estlund and Michael Wachter (Northampton, MA: Edward Elgar, 2013), 463–90, here 470–71.

48. See John Stuart Mill, *Principles of Political Economy*, edited by J. M. Robson (Toronto: University of Toronto Press, 1965), vol. 3 of *Collected Works of John Stuart Mill*, ch. 7, for a classic defense in the liberal tradition. For a contemporary economic view, see Samuel Bowles, Herbert Gintis, and Bo Gustafsson, eds., *Markets and Democracy: Participation, Accountability, and Efficiency* (Cambridge: Cambridge University Press, 1993).

49. See Henry Hansmann, "Employee Ownership of Firms," in *The New Palgrave Dictionary of Economics and Law*, edited by Peter Newman, vol. 2 (London: MacMillan, 1998), 43–47, here 45–46. I thank Steve Nayak-Young for this reference.

50. Gerald Mayer, *Union Membership Trends in the U.S.* (Washington, D.C.: Congressional Research Service, 2004), iv, http://digitalcommons.ilr.cornell.edu/cgi/viewcontent.cgi?article=1176&context=key_workplace.

51. U.S. Bureau of Labor Statistics, *Union Members—2014*, USDL-15-0072 (2015), 1, http://www.bls.gov/news.release/pdf/union2.pdf.

52. By contrast, in Europe, unions often deliver benefits to workers across entire industries, and often to workers as a whole, even when their membership is only a small proportion of all workers. For international comparisons, see Jelle Visser, *ICTWSS: Database on Institutional Characteristics of Trade Unions, Wage Setting, State Intervention and Social Pacts in 51 Countries Between 1960 and 2014* (Amsterdam: Amsterdam Institute for Advanced Labour Studies (AIAS), 2013), http://www.uva-aias.net/en/ictwss.

53. It does not follow that nonunionized firms are free from monopoly. Monopsonistic conditions are pervasive in labor markets. Alan Manning, *Monopsony in Motion: Imperfect Competition in Labor Markets* (Princeton, NJ: Princeton University Press, 2003).
54. Richard B. Freeman and Joel Rogers, *What Workers Want* (Ithaca, NY: ILR Press; New York: Russell Sage Foundation, 2006), 84.
55. For a brief introduction to Germany's system of works councils, see Rebecca Page, *Co-Determination in Germany: A Beginners' Guide* (Düsseldorf: Hans-Böckler-Stiftung, 2009).

Chapter 3

1. Rachel Foxley, *The Levellers: Radical Political Thought in the English Revolution* (Manchester, UK: Manchester University Press, 2013), 1. Since this comment was written, a new account of the Levellers, scholarly and politically engaged, has appeared: John Rees, *The Leveller Revolution* (London: Verso, 2016).
2. Andrew Sharp, ed., *The English Levellers* (Cambridge: Cambridge University Press, 1998), 103.
3. Sharp, ed. *English Levellers*, 136; Alan Houston, "'A Way of Settlement': The Levellers, Monopolies and the Public Interest," *History of Political Thought* 14, no. 3 (1993): 381–420.
4. Thomas L. Leng, "'His Neighbours Land Mark': William Sykes and the Campaign for 'Free Trade' in Civil War England," *Historical Research*, 86 (2013): 230–52.
5. Sharp, ed., *English Levellers*, 94.

6. Sharp, ed., *English Levellers*, 171–72. No one could be elected to two parliaments in succession, no person receiving public money could be elected, and "if any lawyer shall at any time be chosen, he shall be incapable of practice as a lawyer during the whole time of that trust." It is clear the Levellers thought it unlikely the English people would elect any lawyers to Parliament.

7. The organizers of the summit located it in the context of celebrations of the anniversary of Magna Carta: "Rally at Runnymede," https://www.opendemocracy.net/rally -at-runnymede-and-join-opposition; Anthony Barnett, *New Statesman*, February 26, 2015, on the "spirit of Rainborough."

8. Speakers at the "Lilburne 400 Conference" held on March 14, 2015, at the Bishopgate Institute in London included several historians who had written on the Levellers, alongside the radical lawyer Geoffrey Robertson, and the politicians Tariq Ali and Jeremy Corbyn MP. It was organized by the Leveller Association: www.leveller.org.uk. Corbyn attended the launch of John Rees's book, *Leveller Revolution*, in November 2016, and see also the article by Edward Vallance in the *Guardian*, August 20, 2015, and for Ali, *Guardian*, February 20, 2015. The original Grand Remonstrance was a denunciation of the personal rule of Charles I produced by the House of Commons. As Vallance notes, more right-wing British politicians have also appealed to the Levellers' libertarian legacies.

9. An optimistic account can be found in John Tosh, *Why History Matters* (Basingstoke, UK: Palgrave Macmillan, 2008). On the other hand, David Armitage and Jo Guldi argue in *The History Manifesto* (Cambridge: Cambridge University Press,

2014) that the potential of recent historical scholarship to influence contemporary decision-making is not being realized. Their arguments and conclusions have been attacked by Deborah Cohen and Peter Mandler: see the debate in *American Historical Review* 120, no. 2 (April 2015): 530–53.

10. Keith Wrightson, *Earthly Necessities in Earthly Necessities: Economic Lives in Early Modern Britain* (New Haven, CT: Yale University Press, 2000), 139. My account of social and economic change is deeply indebted to this book.

11. Wrightson, *Earthly Necessities*, 226.

12. For a comprehensive study of the social and political implications of the poor law, see Steve Hindle, *On the Parish? The Micro-politics of Poor Relief in Rural England c. 1550–1750* (Oxford: Clarendon Press, 2004).

13. For the army, see Ian Gentles, *The New Model Army in England, Ireland and Scotland* (Oxford: Blackwell, 1992).

14. For Rainborough and Walwyn, see *The Oxford Dictionary of National Biography*; and for Walwyn's 1652 paper defending opponents of the Levant Company and delivered to the Council of State, see *The Writings of William Walwyn*, edited by J. R. McMichael and Barbara Taft (Athens: University of Georgia Press, 1989), 446–52.

15. Sharp, ed., *English Levellers*, 130, 170. The visionary and failed merchant Digger leader, Gerrard Winstanley, also had a profound hostility to wage labor, writing that he had been inspired by God to lead an experiment to work collectively on the common lands of Surrey—"to eat my bread with the sweat of my brows, without either giving hire, or taking hire, looking upon the land as freely mine as an-others": *The Complete Works of Gerrard Winstanley*, edited by Thomas Corns, Ann Hughes, and David Loewenstein

(Oxford: Oxford University Press, 2009), I, 517 (*The New Law of Righteousnes*).

16. Foxley, *The Levellers*; Ann Hughes, "The English Revolution," in David Parker, ed., *Revolutions and Revolutionary Traditions in the West*, (London: Routledge, 2000), 34–52.

17. Barbara Taft, "Walwyn, William (bap. 1600, d. 1681)," in *Oxford Dictionary of National Biography* (Oxford: Oxford University Press, 2004).

18. Craig Muldrew, *The Economy of Obligation: The Culture of Credit and Social Relations in Early Modern England* (Basingstoke, UK: Palgrave Macmillan, 1998), 150–51, is quoted. Karl Polanyi, *The Great Transformation: The Political and Economic Origins of Our Time* (Boston: Beacon Press, 2001), first published 1944, insists on the political and social constructions of "the market." See also Alexandra Shepard, *Accounting for Oneself: Worth, Status and the Social Order in Early Modern England* (Oxford: Oxford University Press, 2015), who stresses the importance of assessments of people's economic worth in social relations within "a pervasive culture of appraisal" (308).

19. Shepard, *Accounting for Oneself*, 278, drawing on Margot Finn, *The Character of Credit: Personal Debt in English Culture, 1740–1914* (Cambridge: Cambridge University Press, 2003).

20. Leng, "His Neighbours Landmark"; Melissa Mowry, "'Commonwealth Wives Who Stand for Their Freedom and Liberty': Leveller Women and the Hermeneutics of Collectivities," *Huntington Library Quarterly*, 77, no. 3 (2014): 305–29; Foxley, *The Levellers*, 143.

21. Andy Wood, *The Politics of Social Conflict: The Peak Country 1520–1770* (Cambridge: Cambridge University Press, 1999), 289–90.

22. My argument is taken from Ann Hughes, "Gender and Politics in Leveller Literature," in *Political Culture and Cultural Politics in Early Modern England*, edited by Susan Amussen and Mark Kishlansky (Manchester, UK: Manchester University Press, 1995), 162–89. It is challenged and qualified by Mowry, "Commonwealth Wives," and Loxley, *The Levellers*.

23. Carole Pateman, *The Disorder of Women: Democracy, Feminism, and Political Theory* (Stanford, CA: Stanford University Press, 1989); Ann Hughes, *Gender and the English Revolution* (London: Routledge, 2011), 145.

24. Indeed, a respectable male-headed household had an advantage in the relationships of credit and trust described by Craig Muldrew.

25. The small farm too is a household rather than an individual enterprise, so it is hard to argue that Paine was proposing an individually based egalitarianism in the American context.

Chapter 4

1. Adam Smith, *An Inquiry into the Nature and Causes of the Wealth of Nations*, edited by R. H. Campbell and A. S. Skinner, 2 vols. (Indianapolis: Glasgow Edition, 1981), vol. 1, 69, http://www.econ.uba.ar/www/institutos/economia/ Ceplad/HPE_Bibliografia_digital/Wealth%20 of%20Nations%20-%20Vol.1.pdf.

2. Roger Lonsdale, ed., *The Poems of Gray, Collins, and Goldsmith* (London: Longman, 1969), 678.

3. Lonsdale, ed., 694.

4. Karl Polanyi, *The Great Transformation* (Boston: Beacon Press, 1968), 72.

5. Polanyi, 73.

Chapter 5

1. Elizabeth Anderson, "What Is the Point of Equality?" *Ethics* 109 (1999): 287–337.
2. With the aid of other work, in a similar vein, that appeared around the same time. Most notably, Samuel Scheffler, "What Is Egalitarianism?" *Philosophy and Public Affairs* 31 (2003): 5–39.
3. Of course, to the extent that the patriarchal family was itself a little firm, or to the extent that the operation was just a sweatshop in what was also a place of residence, there was government even in the tenements. For the required contrast, we have to imagine that piecework, perhaps contrary to fact, wasn't like this. This makes the thought experiment no longer so "natural."
4. Frederick Winslow Taylor, *The Principles of Scientific Management* (New York and London: Harper & Brothers, 1911).
5. R. H. Coase, "The Nature of the Firm," *Economica* 4 (1937): 386–405.
6. Granted, this worry may not be limited to the firm. A monopsonist might threaten to refuse to do business with an independent artisan, unless he votes for his candidate. But, at very least, the worry is not a worry about compensation, conditions, or security. It's a worry instead about the relations of power between laborers and those buying the labor, or its fruits.
7. Charles de Secondat, Baron de Montesquieu, *The Spirit of the Laws*, translated and edited by Anne M. Cohler, Basia C. Miller, and Harold S. Stone (Cambridge: Cambridge University Press, 1989); Lon Fuller, *The Morality of Law* (New Haven, CT: Yale University Press, 1964).

8. Jean-Jacques Rousseau, *The Social Contract and Other Later Political Writings*, translated and edited by Victor Gourevitch (Cambridge: Cambridge University Press, 1997).

9. Minimizing the low costs of exile: "Exile . . . can have severe collateral consequences. The vast majority have no realistic option but to try to immigrate to another communist dictatorship" (38). "Alternatively, their claim might be that where the only sanctions for disobedience are exile, or a civil suit, authority does not exist. That would come as a surprise to those subject to the innumerable state regulations that are backed only by civil sanctions. Nor would a state regulation lack authority if the only sanction for violating it were to force one out of one's job. Finally, managers have numerous other sanctions at their disposal besides firing and suing: they can and often do demote employees; cut their pay; assign them inconvenient hours or too many or too few hours; assign them more dangerous, dirty, menial, or grueling tasks; increase their pace of work; set them up to fail; and, within very broad limits, humiliate and harass them" (55). "Laissez-faire liberals, touting the freedom of the free market, told workers: choose your Leviathan. That is like telling the citizens of the Communist bloc of Eastern Europe that their freedom could be secured by a right to emigrate to any country—as long as they stayed behind the Iron Curtain" (60). "Freedom of entry and exit from any employment relation is not sufficient to justify the outcome" (61). Minimizing consent: "Perhaps the thought is that where consent mediates the relationship between the parties, the relationship cannot be one of subordination to authority" (55). Minimizing the regulation of employment by democratically enacted

law: "What, then, determines the scope and limits of the employer's authority, if it is not a meeting of minds of the parties? The state does so, through a complex system of laws. . . . The *state* has established the constitution of the government of the workplace: it is a form of private government" (53–54).

Chapter 6

1. For two looks at monopsony, see William M. Boal and Michael R. Ransom, "Monopsony in the Labor Market," *Journal of Economic Literature* 35, no. 1 (1997): 86–112 and Orley C. Ashenfelter, Henry Farber, and Michael R. Ransom, "Modern Models of Monopsony in Labor Markets," IZA Discussion Paper No. 4915 (2010). On Walmart, see Alessandro Bonnanno and Rigoberto A. Lopez, "Is Wal-Mart a Monopsony? Evidence from Local Labor Markets," Working paper (2009). For a look at why the monopsony model has not won over most economists, most of all as an explanation of medium- to long-run phenomena, see Peter Kuhn, "Is Monopsony the Right Way to Model Labor Markets? A Review of Alan Manning's *Monopsony in Motion*," *International Journal of the Economics of Business* 11, no. 3 (2004): 369–78.
2. On the wage premium from larger firms, see Brianna Cardiff-Hicks, Francine Lafontaine, and Kathryn Shaw, "Do Large Modern Retailers Pay Premium Wages?" National Bureau of Economic Research Working Paper 20313 (2014).
3. For analyses of some related scenarios under monopsony, see Kip Viscusi, "Union, Labor Market Structure, and the Welfare Implications of the Quality of Work," *Journal of*

Labor Research 1, no. 1 (1980): 175–92; Alison L. Booth and Gylfi Zoega, "Why Do Firms Invest in General Training? 'Good' Firms and 'Bad' Firms as a Source of Monopsony Power," Unpublished manuscript (2000); and Francis Green, Stephen Machin, and Alan Manning, "The Employer Size-Wage Effect: Can Dynamic Monopsony Provide an Explanation?" *Oxford Economic Papers* 48 (1996): 433–55.
4. If Anderson really thinks more job perks is the way to go, she could argue for higher taxes on worker incomes to bring about that end. Furthermore, she might want to oppose the Earned Income Tax Credit and other policies that subsidize pecuniary wages and likely lower the quality of workplace perks (the employer may lower perks to capture more of the value of the subsidy for the firm, rather than it going to the worker).
5. See, for instance, Sanford J. Grossman and Oliver D. Hart, "The Costs and Benefits of Ownership: A Theory of Vertical and Lateral Integration," *Journal of Political Economy* 94, no. 4 (1986): 691–719 and also Oliver D. Hart and John Moore, "Property Rights and the Nature of the Firm," *Journal of Political Economy* 98, no. 6 (1990): 1119–58.
6. A starting point here is Supreet Kaur, Michael Kremer, and Sendhil Mullainathan. "Self-Control at Work," *Journal of Political Economy* 123, no. 6 (2015): 1227–77.
7. See Harvey Silvergate, *Three Felonies a Day: How the Feds Target the Innocent* (New York: Encounter Books, 2011).
8. On some of these mechanisms, see Richard B. Freeman, Douglas Kruse, and Joseph Blasi, "Monitoring Colleagues at Work: Profit Sharing, Employee Ownership, Broad-Based Stock Options and Workplace Performance in the United States," CEP Discussion Paper No. 647 (2004).

9. See, for instance, Ben Craig and John Pencavel, "The Behavior of Worker Cooperatives: The Plywood Companies of the Pacific Northwest," *American Economic Review* 82, no. 5 (1992): 1083–1105.

10. Gary Gorton and Frank Schmid, "Class Struggle inside the Firm: A Study of German Codetermination," Federal Reserve Bank of St. Louis Working Paper (2002).

Chapter 7

1. Debra Satz, comparing classical with neoclassical economists, draws up a similar set of contrasts as I do between early pro-market advocates and nineteenth-century laissez-faire theorists. "[A]lmost everything that the classical economists considered of interest in economic life—in particular their crucial insights into the social effects of different markets on human capacities and social relationships and the ways that different markets are socially embedded—has been omitted" from the models and evaluative standards of neoclassical economics. Debra Satz, *Why Some Things Should Not Be for Sale: The Moral Limits of Markets* (Oxford and New York: Oxford University Press, 2010), 61. Smith, in particular, has been misread as a theorist of benign "invisible hand" self-interest and socially disembedded, self-equilibrating markets. Bromwich rightly invokes Polanyi against such illusions, but wrongly supposes that Smith held them. For corrections, see Gavin Kennedy, "Adam Smith: Some Popular Uses and Abuses," in *Adam Smith: His Life, Thought, and Legacy*, edited by Ryan Hanley (Princeton, NJ: Princeton University Press, 2016), 461–77.

2. Adam Smith, *An Inquiry into the Nature and Causes of the Wealth of Nations, Vol. 1*, Glasgow Edition of the Works and

Correspondence of Adam Smith (Indianapolis: Liberty Fund, 1981), I.10.2.61. Nor did Locke support unregulated labor markets. Although he prescribed harsh measures for dealing with those among the poor whom he imagined to be voluntarily unemployed, he also argued that property owners should be required to hire the involuntarily unemployed at a state-prescribed minimum wage. John Locke, "An Essay on the Poor Law," *Locke: Political Essays*, edited by Mark Goldie (Cambridge: Cambridge University Press, 1997), 188.

3. Elizabeth Anderson, "Ethical Assumptions of Economic Theory: Some Lessons from the History of Credit and Bankruptcy," *Ethical Theory and Moral Practice* 7 (2004): 347–60.

4. Bromwich supposes that Locke supported enclosure on the ground that those excluded were not possessive individualists. This reading, probably derived from C. B. Macpherson, *The Political Theory of Possessive Individualism: Hobbes to Locke* (Oxford: Clarendon Press, 1962), fails to distinguish Locke's justification for unilateral enclosure of the commons in the state of nature from his views of what was permitted once a state is established. Locke argued that, whereas unilateral enclosure of the (open-access) commons in the state of nature was permissible because it would leave enough and as good for others, this was not true for the (jointly communally owned) commons in England. The latter were justly held in common by joint agreement of community members. No individual could unilaterally abrogate that agreement. See Locke, *Second Treatise*, §35. Locke supported people's aspirations to self-employment on the same basis that Lincoln did: all the "vacant" land in America was available to anyone willing to mix their

labor with it. *Second Treatise,* §36. In practice, this position had grievous consequences for Native Americans, and implementing it was inextricable from genocidal racism. However, Locke mistakenly held that privatizing the supposedly uncultivated land in America would redound to everyone's interests, including that of Native Americans. He did not appeal to racist premises to justify his position. On this point, see Jeremy Waldron, *God, Locke, and Equality: Christian Foundations of John Locke's Political Thought* (Cambridge and New York: Cambridge University Press, 2002), Kindle loc. 2256–2335, 2402–15.

5. Adam Smith, *An Inquiry into the Nature and Causes of the Wealth of Nations, Vol. 2,* Glasgow Edition of the Works and Correspondence of Adam Smith (Indianapolis: Liberty Fund, 1981), V.1.f.61.

6. Locke contradicted himself on this point. Notoriously, he invested in the slave trade, and probably helped draft *The Fundamental Constitutions of Carolina,* 1669, http:// avalon.law.yale.edu/17th_century/nc05.asp, which upheld slavery. However, there is no way to reconcile the actual institution of chattel slavery with his theory of property. Although he allowed the traditional justification for slavery— punishment in lieu of execution for combatants in an unjust war—this principle could never justify enslaving noncombatants, particularly not the passing of slave status from mothers to children. See Locke, *Second Treatise,* ch. IV, and the nuanced discussion of Locke on slavery in Waldron, *God, Locke, and Equality,* ch. 7.

7. Hence he also had no answer to Bromwich's challenge, regarding market-dominating firms such as Google or Apple. Smith supposed that states were needed to create

monopolies. He never imagined that increasing returns to scale would create natural monopolies or oligopolies.

8. I will not discuss what's bad about occupying the superior position, although this is an interesting question in its own right. Egalitarians have things to say about it, regarding the corruptions of character and deprivations of the goods of relating to others as equals, entailed by superior status.

9. I'll set aside the "passive-aggressive, that's-not-how-you-do-it-but-far-be-it-from-me-to-interfere father-in-law" in the tenement. He *is* bossing his daughter-in-law around, even if he pretends not to, and even though he lacks the formal authority to do so.

10. Erik Loomis, "This Day in Labor History: December 28, 1973," *Lawyers, Guns & Money*, December 28, 2015, http://www.lawyersgunsmoneyblog.com/2015/12/this-day-in-labor-history-december-28-1972.

11. Simon Head, "Worse Than Wal-Mart: Amazon's Sick and Secret History of Ruthlessly Intimidating Workers," *Salon*, February 23, 2014, http://www.salon.com/2014/02/23/worse_than_wal_mart_amazons_sick_brutality_and_secret_history_of_ruthlessly_intimidating_workers/.

12. Spencer Soper, "Inside Amazon's Warehouse," *Morning Call*, August 17, 2015, http://www.mcall.com/news/local/amazon/mc-allentown-amazon-complaints-20110917-story.html.

13. Head, "Worse than Wal-Mart: Amazon's Sick and Secret History of Ruthlessly Intimidating Workers."

14. Only after suffering from bad publicity and customer complaints about how it treated its workers did Amazon improve ventilation at its warehouses. Corporate reputation and customer satisfaction matters, but workers'

health doesn't. Spencer Soper and Scott Kraus, "Amazon Gets Heat over Warehouse," *Morning Call*, September 25, 2011, http://www.mcall.com/news/local/amazon/mc-allentown-amazon-folo-20110917-story.html. It is worth noting that Amazon's abuses of workers reach deep into their white-collar ranks. See Jodi Kantor and David Streitfeld, "Inside Amazon: Wrestling Big Ideas in a Bruising Workplace," *New York Times*, August 15, 2015, http://www.nytimes.com/2015/08/16/technology/inside-amazon-wrestling-big-ideas-in-a-bruising-workplace.html?_r=0. Although my replies focus on the bottom half of workers, who face the worst conditions, many in the top half also suffer from domination at work.

15. Adam Smith, *The Theory of Moral Sentiments*, edited by D. D. Raphael and A. L. Macfie, Glasgow Edition of the Works and Correspondence of Adam Smith (Oxford: Oxford University Press, 1976), II.3.1.5.

16. Contra Cowen, the rule of law does not mean every infraction should be punished. The optimal degree of enforcement for nearly all laws is vastly less than 100 percent.

17. Ehrenreich, *Nickel and Dimed: On (not) Getting by in America*.

18. Social Security Administration, Measures of Central Tendency for Wage Data, https://www.ssa.gov/oact/cola/central.html, reports a median net compensation for U.S. workers of $28,851.21 in 2014, the latest data available.

19. Saru Jayaraman, *Forked: A New Standard for American Dining* (New York: Oxford University Press, 2016).

20. U.S. Department of Labor, *US Labor Department Seeks Enforcement of Subpoena Issued to Forever 21* (Washington, D.C., 2012), https://www.dol.gov/opa/media/press/whd/WHD20121989.htm#.UIrdYfmfG3l.

21. Oxfam America, *No Relief: Denial of Bathroom Breaks in the Poultry Industry*, 2–3.

22. Marc Linder, *Void Where Prohibited Revisited : The Trickle-Down Effect of OSHA's at-Will Bathroom-Break Regulation* (Iowa City, IA: Fănpìhuà Press, 2003).

23. Hertel-Fernandez and Secunda, "Citizens Coerced: A Legislative Fix for Workplace Political Intimidation Post-Citizens United," 6.

24. U.S. Government Accountability Office, *Enhancing OSHA's Records Audit Process Could Improve the Accuracy of Worker Injury and Illness Data* (Washington, D.C., 2009), 22, https://coreyrobin.files.wordpress.com/2012/05/gao -report-on-osha-october-2009.pdf.

25. Ibid., 24.

26. Susan Lambert, Peter Fugiel, and Julia Henly, *Precarious Work Schedules among Early-Career Employees in the U.S.: A National Snapshot* (Chicago: University of Chicago, EINet, 2014), 13, 7, https://ssascholars.uchicago.edu/sites/default /files/work-scheduling-study/files/lambert.fugiel.henly_.pre carious_work_schedules.august2014_0.pdf. See also María Enchautegui, *Nonstandard Work Schedules and the Well-Being of Low-Income Families* (Washington, D.C.: Urban Institute, 2013), http://www.urban.org/sites/default/files/alfresco /publication-pdfs/412877-Nonstandard-Work-Schedules-and -the-Well-being-of-Low-Income-Families.PDF.

27. Alyssa Figueroa, "The Ugly Walmart Truth: Some Managers Treat Workers Like Dirt," *Alternet*, January 29, 2015, http://www.alternet.org/labor/ugly-walmart-truth-some -managers-treat-workers-dirt.

28. U.S. Department of State, "2014 Trafficking in Persons Report" (2014), https://www.state.gov/j/tip/rls/tiprpt/coun tries/2014/226844.htm.

29. Colleen Owens, Meredith Dank, Justin Breaux, Isela Bañuelos, Amy Farrell, Rebecca Pfeffer, et al., *Understanding the Organization, Operation, and Victimization Process of Labor Trafficking in the United States* (Boston: Urban Institute, Northeastern University, 2014), xii; Jessica Garrison, Ken Bensinger, and Jeremy Singer-Vine, "The New American Slavery: Invited to the U.S., Foreign Workers Find a Nightmare," *Buzzfeed News*, July 24, 2015, http://www.buzzfeed.com/jessicagarrison/the-new-american-slavery-invited-to-the-us-foreign-workers-f.

30. U.S. Department of State, "2014 Trafficking in Persons Report."

31. Garrison, Bensinger, and Singer-Vine, "The New American Slavery: Invited to the U.S., Foreign Workers Find a Nightmare."

32. David Autor, David Dorn, and Gordon Hanson, "The China Syndrome: Local Labor Market Effects of Import Competition in the United States," *American Economic Review* 103, no. 6 (2013): http://dx.doi.org/10.1257/aer.103.6.2121.

33. Elizabeth Anderson, "Values, Risks, and Market Norms," *Philosophy and Public Affairs* 17 (1988): 54–65.

34. David Dayen, "The True Cost: Why the Private Prison Industry Is about So Much More than Prisons," *Talking Points Memo*, August 18, 2016, http://talkingpointsmemo.com/features/privatization/two/.

35. U.S. Office of the Inspector General, *Review of the Federal Bureau of Prisons' Monitoring of Contract Prisons* (Washington, D.C., 2016), 65, https://oig.justice.gov/reports/2016/e1606.pdf.

36. Kim Bobo, *Wage Theft in America: Why Millions of Working Americans Are Not Getting Paid—And What We Can Do About It*, rev. ed. (New York: New Press, 2011), Kindle loc. 259–72.

37. Ibid., Kindle loc. 283–84.

38. Brady Meixell and Ross Eisenbrey, *An Epidemic of Wage Theft Is Costing Workers Hundreds of Millions of Dollars a Year*, Issue Brief #385 (Washington, D.C.: Economic Policy Institute, 2014), http://s3.epi.org/files/2014/wage-theft.pdf.

39. Seymour Drescher, *The Mighty Experiment: Free Labor Versus Slavery in British Emancipation* (Oxford and New York: Oxford University Press, 2002), 132–34.

40. Larry Fauver and Michael Fuerst, "Does Good Corporate Governance Include Employee Representation?: Evidence from German Corporate Boards," *Journal of Financial Economics* 82, no. 3 (2006): 673–710; John Addison, Claus Schnabel, and Joachim Wagner, "Works Councils in Germany: Their Effects on Establishment Performance," *Oxford Economic Papers* 53 (2001): 659–94; Simon Renaud, "Dynamic Efficiency of Supervisory Board Codetermination in Germany," *Labour* 21, nos. 4/5 (2007): 689–712; Felix R. FitzRoy and Kornelius Kraft, "Co-Determination, Efficiency, and Productivity," IZA Discussion Paper Series, No. 1442 (2004), http://hdl.handle.net/10419/20741; Steffen Mueller, "The Productivity Effect of Non-Union Representation," BGPE Discussion Paper No. 74 (2009), http://hdl.handle.net/10419/73422.

41. Brad Delong, "Hoisted from the Archives: A Non-Socratic Dialogue on Social Welfare Functions" (Brad DeLong's Semi-Daily Journal, 2009), http://delong.typepad.com/sdj/2009/04/hoisted-from-the-archives-a-non-socratic-dialogue-on-social-welfare-functions.html.

Contributors

Elizabeth Anderson is Arthur F. Thurnau Professor and John Dewey Distinguished University Professor of Philosophy and Women's Studies at the University of Michigan. She is the author of *The Imperative of Integration* (Princeton), *Value in Ethics and Economics*, and many articles on egalitarianism, democracy, and market society.

David Bromwich is Sterling Professor of English at Yale. He has written on politics and culture for *Dissent, The Nation, The New York Review of Books,* and other journals. He is the author of several books including, most recently, *The Intellectual Life of Edmund Burke: From the Sublime and Beautiful to American Independence.*

Tyler Cowen holds the Holbert L. Harris Chair of Economics at George Mason University and is a Professor in Economics at the Center for the Study of Public Choice. He is also the Director of the Mercatus Center. He writes for the economics blog, Marginal Revolution. He is the author most recently of *The Complacent Class: The Self Defeating Quest for the American Dream.*

Ann Hughes is recently retired from Keele University in the United Kingdom, where she was Professor of Early Modern History since 1995, and Director of the Research Institute for the Humanities and Research Director for the Humanities and Social Sciences from 2012–2014. She is the author most recently of *Gender and the English Revolution* (Routledge, 2011).

Niko Kolodny is Professor of Philosophy at the University of California, Berkeley. Prior to that he was Assistant Professor of Philosophy at Harvard University and Research Associate at the Research School of Social Sciences of the Australian National University. His main interests lie in moral and political philosophy.

Stephen Macedo is the Laurance S. Rockefeller Professor of Politics at the University Center for Human Values at Princeton University, where he has also been the Founding Director of the Program on Law and Public Affairs (1999–2001), and Director of the University Center for Human Values (2001–2009). His books include *Liberal Virtues: Citizenship, Virtue, and Community in Liberal Constitutionalism* (Oxford University, 1990); *Diversity and Distrust: Civic Education in a Multicultural Democracy* (Harvard University, 2000); the co-authored *Democracy at Risk: How Political Choices Undermine Citizen Participation, and What We Can Do About It* (Brookings Institution Press, 2005); and *Just Married: Same-Sex Couples, Monogamy, and the Future of Marriage* (Princeton University Press, 2015).

Index

Adams, Abigail, 42

Adams, John, on government as "everywhere," 42–43

Affordable Care Act (ACA [2010]), 49, 111

Agreement of the People, 7, 77–78, 83

Alchian, Armen, 54–57; on a firm's lack of power and authority, 54–55; on sanctions against employees, 55

Alexander v. FedEx Ground Package System (2014), 159n26

Ali, Tariq, 78, 166n8

Amazon, poor treatment of workers at, 128–30, 177–78n14

American Civil War, and the universalization of independent labor, 32

anarchism, 6

Anderson, Elizabeth, viii, ix, xvii–xviii, 89–90, 112; on Cowen's skewed view of working conditions and wages in the United States, 134–35; critique of her views on early modern economic and social change in England, 80–88; focus of on quasi-political relations of government between employees and employers, 101; fundamental objections of to private government, 127; on hierarchies of authority, xi–xii; on the modern industrial firm as "private government" and a "dictatorship," x–xi, 38; onprivate business firms as "communist dictatorships in our midst," 39, 108–9; Tanner lectures of, 78; on ways to increase worker protections against arbitrary treatment, xii

Anglican Church, 11; as a form of monopoly, 16; private government functions of, 8–9

Grossman, Sanford, 113
guilds, 82; abolition of guild monopolies, 14; guild government, 14, 150n37; private court system of, 9

Hammond, James, 30
Hart, Oliver, 113
hemiagnosia: institutional hemiagnosia, 65; political hemiagnosia, 58
Holland, 13, 14
Homestead Act (1862), 31, 124
Hughes, Ann, xiii, 119, 125; on the rise of market society, 121–22

immigration/immigrants, 32–33, 137; immigration rights, 159n23
Imperative of Integration, The (Anderson), viii
independent contractors, 51, 132; employees as independent contractors, 57, 159n26
individualism, 65
Industrial Revolution, the, vii, ix, 48; centralized production as a product of, 65; and the change from egalitarian values to support for workplace authoritarianism, 61–62; and the divide between pre-and post–Industrial Revolution pro-market theory, 120–26; as a fundamental turning point in egalitarian social thought, 6; and the movement of paid work from the household to the factory, 49; and the pervasiveness of markets in

labor, 36; pre–Industrial Revolution market-friendly ideology, 122–23; as shattering the egalitarian ideal of universal self-government, 33–36
industrialization. *See* urban industrialization
inequality, dimensions of (authority, esteem, and standing), 3–4, 91, 98; example of authority inequality, 127–28; example of esteem and standing inequalities at Amazon, 128–30
inflation, during the Revolutionary War, 25
institutions: spread of across society in the nineteenth century, 34–35; total institutions, 62

Jensen, Michael, 56
Johnson, Thomas, 7
joint-stock corporations, 21, 152n56
journeymen, 23, 33–34, 82
justice, xviii, 78, 151n46; distributive justice, xix, 8, 59, 120, 148n15

Kolodny, Niko, xv–xvi, 119–20; rejection of the rule of law as an illusion, 130; on subjection to authority, 126–27

labor: as a commodity, xiv, 2, 97–98, 120, 124; free labor, 35; labor shortages, 27; marginalized nature of academic research concerning, 135; migrant labor,

THE UNIVERSITY CENTER FOR HUMAN VALUES SERIES
STEPHEN MACEDO, EDITOR

Multiculturalism and "The Politics of Recognition" by Charles Taylor

A Matter of Interpretation: Federal Courts and the Law by Antonin Scalia

Freedom of Association edited by Amy Gutmann

Work and Welfare by Robert M. Solow

The Lives of Animals by J. M. Coetzee

Truth v. Justice: The Morality of Truth Commissions edited by Robert I. Rotberg and Dennis Thompson

Goodness and Advice by Judith Jarvis Thomson

Human Rights as Politics and Idolatry by Michael Ignatieff

Democracy, Culture and the Voice of Poetry by Robert Pinsky

Primates and Philosophers: How Morality Evolved by Frans de Waal

Striking First: Preemption and Prevention in International Conflict by Michael W. Doyle

Meaning in Life and Why It Matters by Susan Wolf

The Limits of Constitutional Democracy edited by Jeffrey K. Tulis and Stephen Macedo

Foragers, Farmers, and Fossil Fuels: How Human Values Evolve by Ian Morris

Private Government: How Employers Rule Our Lives (and Why We Don't Talk about It) by Elizabeth Anderson